GREEK TRAGEDY

AN INTRODUCTION

Originally published in 1986 as *Die griechische Tragödie,* © Artemis
Verlag München und Zürich, Verlagsort München.

English translation © 1991 The Johns Hopkins University Press
All rights reserved. Published 1991
Printed in the United States of America on acid-free paper

Second printing, paperback, 1993

The Johns Hopkins University Press
2715 North Charles Street
Baltimore, Maryland 21218-4319
The Johns Hopkins Press Ltd., London

Library of Congress Cataloging-in-Publication Data

Zimmermann, Bernhard.
[Griechische Tragödie. English]
Greek tragedy : an introduction / Bernhard Zimmermann ;
translated by Thomas Marier.
p. cm.
Includes bibliographical references and index.
ISBN 0-8018-4118-6 (alk. paper). — ISBN 0-8018-4119-4
(pbk. : alk. paper)
1. Greek drama (Tragedy)—History and criticism. I. Title.
PA3131.Z513 1991 882'.0109—dc20 90-45561

A catalog record for this book is available from the British Library.

CONTENTS

CONTENTS

GREEK TRAGEDY

AN INTRODUCTION

I

INTRODUCTION

Canonization and Survival

In Aristophanes' *Frogs*, which was produced in 405 B.C., the god Dionysus descends to the underworld with the intention of restoring to Athens his favorite poet, Euripides, who had died the year before. On his arrival, he finds Hades in a state of turmoil: Euripides is challenging Aeschylus's right to the tragic throne in the underworld (Sophocles, in contrast, who had died shortly after Euripides, lays no claim to this honor). Dionysus presides over the contest that is to determine which of the two poets should be accorded this prestigious seat. The debate lasts for several rounds, in which both offer exquisite samples of their art. Yet Dionysus, despite his preference for Euripides, is neither willing nor able to reach a decision on the basis of aesthetic criteria. It is only after each is required to give his expert opinion on Athenian politics, to recommend the best course of action for the polis in its present desperate situation, that Aeschylus prevails. In a festive procession, the victorious poet is escorted back to the upper world so that in the future Athens may profit from his political advice.

This thumbnail sketch of the plot of *Frogs* throws light

2

GREEK TRAGEDY

on several points which form the backdrop, so to speak, against which Greek tragedy must be understood: the connection between the god Dionysus and the theater, that is, the performance of both comedies and tragedies; the reciprocal relation of politics and art in fifth-century Athens; the dramatic performance as *agōn* ('contest'), reflected in the conflict between Aeschylus and Euripides as well as in Dionysus's role as judge; and, finally, the reduction of the mass of tragic poets to three names: Aeschylus, Sophocles, and Euripides.

Let us begin with this last fact. From *Frogs* it is clear that the canonization of these three poets was not the result of a chance process of survival, but was already fixed in the year 405 B.C. — only one year after the deaths of Euripides and Sophocles and some fifty years after that of Aeschylus. A law of 386 B.C., which permitted the revival of old tragedies (a similar law applying to the plays of Aeschylus seems to have been passed in 456 B.C.) and thereby elevated the works of the three great tragedians to the status of "classics," was only the official confirmation of what was already settled in the mind of every Athenian spectator by 405 B.C. Thus, the canonization of their plays can be explained easily as a consequence of popular taste, the judgment of fellow dramatists, and the theatrical practice of the fourth century.

Of the great many other tragic poets, most are known to us only as names; we possess little more than scanty particulars about their lives and insubstantial fragments from their plays, so that it is hardly possible to form a picture of their work. According to an ancient tradition known to us from the *Ars Poetica* of Horace, it was Thespis who "invented" tragic poetry and traveled throughout Attica performing plays on his "theatrical cart" (275f.). It is indeed conceivable that Thespis played an important role in the development of the Great Dionysia, the dramatic festival that formed part of the new "cultural policy" of the tyrant Peisistratus (see pp. 8–9).

We know more about Choerilus and Phrynichus, who wrote tragedies in the late sixth and early fifth centuries. Choerilus, according to our sources, made his debut as a tragic poet between 523 and 520 B.C. and was still active in 468 B.C., when he was Sophocles' rival in the tragic competition. The two quotations that survive from his considerable corpus of some 160 plays indicate that his diction was highly refined and rich in metaphor.

Phrynichus, too, was already active by the end of the sixth century and is important for the history of the genre in that he was the first tragic poet to bring contemporary history onto the Attic stage. His *Capture of Miletus* and *Phoenician Women* antedate Aeschylus's *Persians* by several years (see pp. 29–30). In Aristophanes' day Phrynichus was still fondly remembered for the music of his choral verse. In *Wasps* (422 B.C.) the chorus enters the orchestra warbling "ancient-honey-Sidon-Phrynichus-lovely" strains, old-fashioned melodies after the manner of Phrynichus (recalling, it would seem, his *Phoenician Women*) that were appealing perhaps on account of their exotic flavor.

Among the contemporaries of Sophocles and Euripides, the poets Ion of Chios and Agathon deserve our attention. Born ca. 485 B.C., Ion not only wrote tragedies but tried his hand at other genres as well: he is supposed to have composed poems of varied content, dithyrambs, hymns, and the first memoirs in world literature, the *Visits* (*Epidemiai*). His style is praised by the anonymous author of the critical treatise *On the Sublime* as "without fault, polished, and elegant," though he lacked the "fire" of Sophocles (33.5).

The parody to which Aristophanes subjects his contemporary Agathon in his *Women at the Thesmophoria* (411 B.C.,) may give us an impression of that tragedian's work. In this comedy Agathon performs a hymn that evinces no relation to the action of the play. A remark in the *Poetics* of Aristotle (1456a 29f.) is consistent with Aristophanes' parody: the philosopher stresses that Agathon was the

4

first not only to compose choral songs bearing no relation to the dramatic action but also, as Aristotle writes in another passage of the *Poetics* (1451b 21), to invent new material instead of drawing on the stock of traditional myths.

The music of Agathon's compositions must have had an uneasy, yet appealing rhythm with frequent and surprising variations (see also pp. 19–20). It also seems that he was given to oversubtle formulation, the coining of new words, and exaggerated antitheses, as the slave who announces the entrance of Agathon in *Women at the Thesmophoria* (49ff.) clearly indicates: "Agathon, the maker of fine verse, our champion, is about to lay the ribs, the foundations of his dramatic ship. He is bending the felloes of new songs, turning his verse here, gluing together melodies there, forging maxims, contrasting rhetorically, molding as of wax, rounding off, pouring forth."*

That we possess in their entirety 7 of the 80 tragedies of Aeschylus, 7 of the 123 of Sophocles, and 19 of the 90 of Euripides is the result of a centuries-long process of selective transmission. When, after 386 B.C., fifth-century plays began to be revived (Euripides was especially popular), directors and actors naturally revised and adapted their scripts to make them conform to their audiences' changing tastes. In time this process would have led inevitably to the contamination of the texts through alteration and interpolation by later hands, had not the orator and statesman Lycurgus, in 330 B.C., seen to the establishment of reliable, official editions of the three tragedians, against which actors were compelled to check their own scripts. In the Hellenistic period, Greek tragedy, and indeed the whole of Greek literature, became the focus of scholarly attention in Alexandria, the cultural center of the age, where, in the magnificent library of the Museum, texts

*Unless otherwise indicated, translations of quotations are by the translator.

were collected and edited. In their efforts to restore the texts to their original state, the Alexandrian scholars compared existing copies, produced new editions, and provided them with commentaries. Alexander of Aetolia (first half of the third century B.C.) and Aristophanes of Byzantium (ca. 257–180 B.C.) worked on the tragic poets; the latter inspected the work of his predecessors, and the short summaries (hypotheseis) appended to many plays derive from him. The basis for the editions of the tragedians was the official copy at Athens, which the Alexandrians had borrowed against an immense security, and never returned. The Alexandrian scholars appear to have included in their selection of texts for annotation those plays that were popular in their own time, and the plays continued to be selected in this manner under the Roman empire. Some editions, for example, included seven plays of Aeschylus, seven of Sophocles, and ten of Euripides. We owe to luck the preservation of nine additional Euripidean tragedies, which were not supplied with commentaries: they formed part of a complete edition arranged in alphabetical order—Helen, Electra, Children of Heracles, Heracles, Suppliant Women, Iphigeneia at Aulis, Iphigeneia among the Taurians, Ion, Cyclops (the Greek titles of these plays all begin with ē, i, or k)—which withstood the test of time in a private collection and was later copied onto a manuscript.

Two periods in Byzantine history were decisive for the transmission of ancient literature. Interest in the poetry of the pagan Greek past waned in the anticultural age of Iconoclasm (A.D. 726–842). It was not until the second half of the ninth century that the literature of antiquity once again became the focus of intense study, engaging the scholars and churchmen in the circle of the patriarch Photius (ca. A.D. 810–ca. 897). The texts that had survived were collected and transcribed in minuscule, the script of that period. This brief interval of vigorous intellectual activity in Constantinople came to an abrupt end with the

invasion of the Crusaders under the misguidance of the
Venetians (A.D. 1204). As a result of this conquest, and of
the later reconquest (A.D. 1261), innumerable works were
lost. The following period was marked by renewed en-
thusiasm for the study of ancient texts. The philologists
Maximus Planudes (ca. A.D. 1250–1310), Thomas Magister
(ca. A.D. 1270–1325), Manuel Moschopulus (ca. A.D. 1265–
1315), and Demetrius Triclinius (ca. A.D. 1280–1340) ap-
proached Greek tragedy from the standpoint of the textual
critic (seeking to establish the "correct" text) and metri-
cian. Like the scholars of the Alexandrian and Roman periods, they too concentrated on a select handful of plays, the
so-called Byzantine triad—that is, three plays of each poet
(Aeschylus: *Prometheus, Seven against Thebes, Persians;*
Sophocles: *Ajax, Electra, Oedipus the King;* Euripides:
Hecuba, Orestes, Phoenician Women). The results of
their diligent research were reflected in the first printed
editions of the sixteenth century and represent the most
significant link between antiquity and the Renaissance.

Tragedy and Cult — Tragedy
and the Polis — Theatrical Conditions

Let us return to Aristophanes' *Frogs.* That is the god Dionysus who decides which of the two poets should occupy
the tragic throne in the underworld, and that his decision
ultimately depends on their political views, illustrate the
connection between tragedy (and comedy) and the cult of
Dionysus as well as the reciprocal relation of poetry and
public life, of tragedy and the polis. Both points are essential to the interpretation of fifth-century tragedy.

The close connection between tragedy and Dionysiac
cult, the masks worn by the actors during the tragic performance, and the term *tragōidia* indicate that the institution of tragedy had preliterary origins. Singing, simple
mimetic representation, and the wearing of masks are

associated with religious celebrations. The meaning of the word *tragōidia* has long been controversial. Of the many suggested renderings, 'song delivered at the sacrifice of a goat' is the most plausible.

Apart from these obscure beginnings in the cult of Dionysus, we have to assume, following Aristotle (*Poetics* 1449a 9–11, 19–21), that the development of tragedy was in some way influenced by other forms of poetry:

> Both tragedy and comedy were originally improvisational (tragedy was developed by those who led the dithyramb, comedy by those who led the phallic processions). . . . With respect to its magnificence: from its beginnings in short traditional tales and a ridiculous style (it is, in fact, an altered form of the satyric) tragedy developed only late into a dignified art. With respect to its meter: the trochaic tetrameter was replaced by the iambic trimeter.

There is indeed a clear connection between tragedy and the dithyramb, which is a kind of choral poetry. Like dithyrambs, choral songs in tragedy often treat mythical subjects, and the dialect used in both is Doric, whereas that of tragic dialogue is elevated Attic. Finally, it is a fair assumption that tragic song developed out of the dithyramb, for both were performed at the festival of Dionysus and the two genres show signs of constant mutual influence in the fifth century. Just what Aristotle meant by "the satyric," however, is disputed. We cannot, of course, simply posit that satyr drama or "satyr dithyramb," if such a genre even existed, were early forms of tragedy. It is more likely that he is using the term in an extended sense. He is probably not referring obliquely to a cultic forerunner of tragedy the nature of which we can no longer grasp.

The historian Herodotus preserves two noteworthy pieces of evidence for the early stages of dramatic poetry. The historian reports (1.23) that, under the tryant Periandes of Corinth, the poet Arion was the first to "compose, name, and produce" the dithyramb. "But since," as F. Graf notes, "Archilochus of Paros had already spoken of the dithyramb a half-century earlier (in connection with the cult of Dionysus), Herodotus can only be referring to a later stage in the development of the genre. When the historian says that Arion 'named' the dithyramb, he must mean that Arion gave titles to his works. These titles probably described subjects that lay outside the small sphere of cult practice and were mythical" (*Griechische Mythologie* [Munich and Zurich, 1985] 140). In another passage (5.67) Herodotus tells us that the Sicyonians used to worship not the god Dionysus but Adrastus, hero of the city, memorializing his sufferings with "tragic choruses." Later the tyrant Cleisthenes, for political reasons (Sicyon was then at war with Argos, and Adrastus was, according to the myth, the son of an Argive king), stripped the local hero of his honors. He transferred the choral song to Dionysus and the sacrifice to Melanippides, a hero whom he himself had introduced from Thebes. Herodotus's notice thus calls attention to another factor in the development of tragedy: politics. A tyrant seeking to secure his power on a religious base transforms an existing hero cult to include performances by tragic choruses in honor of the god Dionysus.

We can trace a similar development at Athens in the second half of the sixth century. The tyrant Peisistratus presumably either introduced the festival of the City Dionysia (also called the Great Dionysia) in honor of Dionysus, whose statue had been relocated to Athens from the rural territory of Eleutherae, or reorganized an older festival and made it especially grand.

Peisistratus's motives were primarily political. By instituting the magnificent five-day festival, the tyrant made Athens the religious center of Attica and diminished the prestige of the local cults under the control of his noble rivals. Like Cleisthenes of Sicyon, Peisistratus probably consecrated the festival to the god Dionysus to win popu-

lar support. It was above all the rural population that
stood behind him when he first came to power in 561 B.C.,
for the farmers had particularly close ties to Dionysus as
a god of fertility and of wine. Moreover, the splendor of the
City Dionysia, in which the urban population, from which
Peisistratus drew much of his backing during the heyday
of his tyranny (546–527 B.C.), took part, affirmed the
tyrant's preeminence in the presence of the other nobles.
The other festival in honor of Dionysus, the Rural Dionysia, had always been celebrated in the country. It was a
lively, earthy celebration with a phallic procession and
amusements such as sack races.

The politicization of the City Dionysia in the late sixth
century helps to explain why the festival was so important
to the fifth-century democracy. After the Persian Wars it
became a political instrument par excellence. The splendor of the festival now served to exalt the Athenians in the
presence of their dependent allies. Ceremonies were incor-
porated into the festival, which, among the Athenians
themselves, promoted a sense of solidarity and, among
the allies, advertised the power of the Athenian empire.
As the allies, who were compelled to pay annual tribute,
sat in the theater of Dionysus and watched, outstanding
Athenians received commendations; the sons of the
Athenian war dead were awarded armor; and the surplus
tribute was brought out for display.

It was above all the tragic competition (agōn), which
was institutionalized as early as 534 B.C., that made the
Great Dionysia such a great attraction. The performance
of tragedies, and later of dithyrambs (from ca. 509 B.C.) and
comedies (from 486 B.C.), was agonistic—that is, a form of
competition among poets.

The Dionysia, and so too the tragic agōn, were organized by the polis. The eponymous archon, the chief
official in the polis, was in charge of the festival. He
selected three poets from all those who had submitted a
tetralogy, that is, three tragedies and one satyr play. For

each of these three dramatic productions the archon also appointed a 'manager' (chorēgos), or wealthy citizen, whose responsibility it was to finance and manage the chorus. This service (chorēgia) was virtually a form of indirect taxation, one of many so-called liturgies, or public duties, to which the wealthy were liable. A poet would then spend the next half year or so rehearsing his play with the actors and the chorus, which consisted of fifteen Athenian citizens. He was thus his own 'producer' (didaskalos). The dramatists seem, as a rule, to have applied "for a chorus"— that is, for the right to produce a play—every two or three years. Two days before the beginning of the festival, in the Attic month of Elaphebolion (March/April), the poet, actors, chorus, and manager were presented to the public, in a ceremonial parade called the proagōn, wearing garlands but without masks or costumes. In the evening of the following day a cult statue of Dionysus was brought into the god's shrine from a spot outside the city walls: this ceremony was a reenactment of the founding of the Dionysia. On the first day of the festival, the tenth of Elaphebolion, which was inaugurated with a solemn procession into the theater of Dionysus and a sacrifice, the dithyrambs were performed. Originally part of the cult of Dionysus, the dithyramb evolved, under the influence of epic and Doric choral lyric, into a narrative, balladlike genre. At the dithyrambic contest the ten tribes, the largest administrative units in democratic Athens, competed against one another, each apparently with fifty-member choruses, one of men and one of boys. The next four days were reserved for the dramatic performances. From 486 B.C. five comedies were performed on the second day, and a tragic tetralogy on each of the remaining three. Aeschylus's trilogies were as a rule thematically related, and even the concluding satyr play dealt with a subject taken from the same mythical cycle; from the time of Sophocles the four plays are often unrelated in theme. The poets were ranked at the conclusion of the competition, not by a panel of experts, but by ten judges chosen by means of a complicated procedure.

Tragic poetry played a subordinate role at the Lenaea, the other festival of Dionysus at which dramatic performances were given. It was held in the month of Gamelion (January/February). Tragic contests were introduced ca. 430 B.C. Comedies, which had always been performed at the Lenaea, were made into a form of competition ca. 440 B.C. This festival was organized by the *archōn basileus*, the magistrate responsible for religious affairs. This fact alone is an indication of its antiquity. Because no regular travel to Athens by sea was possible in January and February, the Athenians celebrated this festival alone, without the lavish display before their non-Athenian allies.

The satyr play counteracted the shock of the foregoing three tragedies and ended the tetralogy on a jovial, conciliatory note. In satyr drama stereotypical plot patterns seem to have been favored, as far as we can generalize on the basis of a regrettably narrow range of material (Euripides' *Cyclops* is the only satyr play that has come down to us intact; we also possess extensive fragments of Sophocles' *Trackers* and Aeschylus's *Net Drawers*). The dramatis personae of satyr drama fall into two groups: Silenus and the chorus of satyrs, and the gods and heroes familiar from tragedy and myth. The presence of satyrs alone indicates that satyr drama is connected with the cult of Dionysus, since satyrs are part of Dionysus's entourage (in tragedy the connection is less obvious). They sport horses' tails and erect phalloi and are led by their father (Pappo-) Silenus, who lacks their bestial attributes. By nature they are at once curious and timid, ostentatious and obsequious. Their antagonists are the gods and heroes, such as Odysseus in Euripides' *Cyclops* or Apollo, Hermes, and the mountain nymph Cyllene in Sophocles' *Trackers*. The peculiar appeal of satyr drama lies in the collision of the world of tragedy—from which the story (*mythos*) of a satyr play is taken and to which some of its dramatis personae belong—with the unheroic, bestial world of the satyrs.

In many satyr plays an important role is played by the villain (Polyphemus in *Cyclops*). The satyrs remain in his clutches until he is finally overcome by a more cunning or more powerful hero (Odysseus in *Cyclops*). Liberated from captivity, they can return to their master Dionysus.

In keeping with the nature of these wild creatures, satyr drama is preoccupied with erotic impulses and gustatory delights. These themes are associated with the cult of Dionysus and are often presented enigmatically, like the objects of the cult itself.

The plays of the fifth century were performed only once. This rule was broken after 456 B.C., when the people voted to allow Aeschylus's plays to be restaged. The revival of old tragedies and satyr plays by other poets was not permitted until 386 B.C. This principle of the unique tragic performance, the agonistic element, whereby the tragedians were constantly in competition with one another, and the rivalry between tragedy and the old "Dionysiac" genre of dithyramb, which was performed at the same festival, contributed to the rapid development of the genre, stimulating formal and artistic as well as technical innovation. Thus, Aeschylus is said to have introduced the second actor, Sophocles the third. The latter is also credited with the introduction of the painted backdrop (*skēnographia*). To the basic choral song (*chorikon*) were added first the antiphonal exchange between the chorus and an actor (*amoibaion*) and later the solo (*monōidia*) and the duet, both of which were sung exclusively by actors and developed into brilliant showpieces of musical virtuosity by Euripides more than any other.

As paradoxical as it may sound, the conditions of the Attic theater also promoted the development of the genre. The plays were performed in the theater of Dionysus on the southern slope of the Acropolis in Athens. The actors occupied a slightly elevated stage (*skēnē*), behind which was a building with as many as three doors, while the

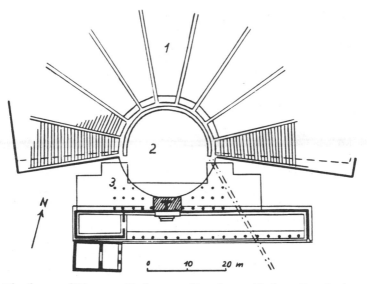

The theater of Dionysus: (1) *theatron*, (2) *orchestra*, (3) *skēnē*. Drawing by C. Newiger, after Dinsmoor, from H.-J. Newiger, "Drama und Theater," in *Das griechische Drama*, ed. G. A. Seeck (Darmstadt, 1979).

chorus sang and danced in the orchestra, that is, on the circular dancing floor between the stage and the rising tiers of seats on which the spectators sat (see the illustration). Because of the simplicity of this arrangement, the stage scenery necessarily left much to the spectators' imagination. Similarly, the two theatrical machines of the Attic stage remind us how far from realistic fifth-century performances were. The *ekkyklēma*, a small trolley that could be wheeled forth through the doors of the stage building, served to represent interiors—tableaux of a sort. The other device was the crane (*geranos* or *mēchanē*), suspended from which the deus ex machina, for which Euripides above all was notorious, might appear. Finally, the masks worn by the actors naturally precluded their representing emotion by means of facial expression.

Accordingly, it was the highly evocative language of tragedy that communicated the feelings of the characters to the audience and created the illusion of a particular setting in the spectator's inner eye. A remarkable example of this process—which Eric W. Handley has aptly called "verbal scene painting" (*The Dyscolus of Menander* [London, 1965] 23)—is the vivid description of the decoration of the temple of Apollo at Delphi in Euripides' *Ion* (184ff.).

The greatest challenge facing the fifth-century Athenian playwright lay in his treatment of what was, by convention, traditional material. The plot of a tragedy was, with few exceptions, drawn from the store of myth. The poet did not invent his stories: historical plays were written only in the early years of the genre and then again in the fourth century, and fictitious ones first by Agathon near the end of the fifth century. Rather, his achievement was measured by the manner in which he elaborated the traditional framework of the myth through the representation of characters and their motives, the emphasis and attenuation of plot elements, the insertion of minor figures—in short, through fresh interpretation of the material supplied by tradition.

It is therefore hardly surprising that the stories of certain mythical houses, such as that of Atreus or Labdacus, were frequently chosen subjects. The poet strove to make his play better than his rivals' versions of the same material. Such literary battles could go on for years, as the plays dealing with the story of Electra show. The audience was anxious to see, not how the play turned out, but rather how the poet brought the action to the conclusion prescribed by the myth.

The Athenian spectator—who himself had taken part in a tragic performance as a member of a chorus (*choreutēs*) and whose attendance at the dramatic festivals had been fostered, presumably from Pericles' day, by the institution of a theoric fund—had firsthand knowledge of the theater and so was able to enjoy and appreciate the poet's constant struggle with its conventions and its myths. The poet, for his part, could take advantage of the spectator's experience by playing on his expectations, by advancing or retarding dramatic events, even by threatening to breach the frame of the story, and then ultimately bringing the action back into congruity with the myth.

Structure, Meter, and Music

In planning out his work the playwright had to consider both the actors and the chorus. For it was the alternation of the parts delivered by these two groups that gave a classical tragedy its characteristic structure, described by Aristotle in the twelfth chapter of his *Poetics*. He draws a distinction between *parodos* ('entrance from the side') and *stasimon* ('standing song'), that is, between the song delivered by the chorus as it filed into the orchestra via passageways at either side of the stage building and any choral song delivered thereafter, while the chorus was dancing in the orchestra. The parodos and stasima in effect divide the play into discrete sections: prologue, episodes, and *exodos*. Aristotle defined the prologue as "the part of a tragedy preceding the entrance of the chorus," the episode as "the part of a tragedy between choral songs," and the exodos as "the part of a tragedy following the last choral song." The prologue is, of course, missing in those plays that open with a parodos, such as Aeschylus's *Persians* and *Suppliants*.

The poet was free to modify this basic structure. He could assign to the chorus a more prominent role in the action by involving it in a lyric dialogue (*kommos* or *amoibaion*) with one or more of the actors. Or he could transfer the lyric element from the orchestra to the stage by having the actors sing arias (monodies) or duets. Sophocles' *Oedipus the King*, which Aristotle regarded as the ideal tragedy, exemplifies the traditional pattern (D = dialogue, S = song, R = recitative):

1–150	*Prologue*
D	(*a*) 1–84. Oedipus–Priests: Thebes is afflicted with a plague. In their plight the priests turn to Oedipus, their only hope.
D	(*b*) 85–150. Creon–Priests: The Delphic oracle indicates that the city can be saved only if Laius's murderer is punished.
151–215	*Parodos*
S	In a hymn the chorus calls on the gods for help.
216–462	*First episode*
D	(*a*) 216–99. Oedipus–chorus leader: a thoroughgoing search for the murderer is under way.
D	(*b*) 300–462. Oedipus–Teiresias–chorus leader (–Youth): The seer discloses the truth: Oedipus is himself the object of the search. The king suspects Teiresias of complicity with the killer.
463–512	*First stasimon*
S	The chorus is at a loss. It declares its support for Oedipus.
513–862	*Second episode*
D	(*a*) 513–630. Creon–Oedipus–chorus leader: Creon is also accused of complicity by Oedipus.
D	(*b*) 631–48. Jocasta–Creon–Oedipus–chorus leader: Jocasta attempts to mediate.
D+S	(*c*) 649–97. Jocasta–Creon–Oedipus–chorus leader (*amoibaion*): Oedipus yields and does not condemn Creon.
D	(*d*) 698–862. Oedipus–Jocasta–chorus leader: Jocasta mentions the oracle and the fork in the road at which Laius was killed. Oedipus surmises that he is Laius's

killer and sends for the sole surviving
eyewitness.

863–910	*Second stasimon*
S	The chorus fears for Oedipus.

911–1085	*Third episode*
D	Jocasta—chorus leader—messenger (from Corinth)—Oedipus: The messenger reports that Polybus, king of Corinth, is dead and tells Oedipus that he is not the son of Polybus and Merope. Jocasta surmises the whole truth. Oedipus is intent on bringing the messenger and the eyewitness face to face so as to be certain about his engendering.

1086–1109	*Third stasimon*
S	The chorus delivers a song of joy.

1110–85	*Fourth episode (peripety)*
D	Oedipus—herdsman—messenger: The truth is revealed.

1186–1222	*Fourth stasimon*
S	The chorus sings of the illusory nature of human happiness.

1223–1530	*Exodos*
D	(a) 1223–96. Messenger—chorus leader: Jocasta has killed herself, and Oedipus has put out his eyes.
D+S+R	(b) 1297–1366. Chorus—Oedipus (*amoibaion*): Ecce homo.
D	(c) 1367–1514. Oedipus—Creon—chorus leader (—Antigone—Ismene): Oedipus sorts things out. He decides to leave Thebes.
R	(d) 1515–30. Chorus—Oedipus (—Antigone—Ismene): Parting words.

A tragedy consists, as the analysis of *Oedipus the King* shows, of alternating sung, recited, and spoken parts. We may gain some sense of the music to which tragic verse was set by studying its various meters.

Ancient verse is quantitative: a line consists of a sequence not of stressed and unstressed syllables, but of shorts (∪) and longs (−), and under certain conditions the syllable can be either long or short (x). Metricians refer to these three signs as breve, longum, and anceps, respectively. A given type of verse is determined by a given scheme of possible combinations of short and long syllables.

The iambic trimeter (x−∪−x−∪−x−∪−) is the meter used for dialogue in Greek tragedy. Passages delivered in recitative are, by contrast, relatively rare. In a fair number of plays (*Persians* or *Agamemnon*, for example) the chorus enters chanting recitative in a meter based on the so-called marching anapaest) (∪∪−). In Aeschylus and in the later works of Euripides, spoken passages are sometimes delivered in trochaic tetrameter (−∪−x−∪−x−∪−x−∪−), a form of recitative associated with scenes of heightened suspense or great moment.

Sung parts were composed in a variety of meters. The poet could choose from the meters of choral and monodic lyric, dithyramb, ritual chant, and popular song. He gave each song a unique metrical (that is, rhythmical and musical) form to evoke in the listener's mind this or that poetic genre. The listener, for his part, was expected to grasp these metrical allusions now to certain songs familiar from everyday life, such as marriage songs or religious hymns, now to compositions from other genres. In Euripides' *Trojan Women*, for example, Cassandra sings the refrain of her aria (308ff.) in aeolics. Traditionally used for marriage songs, this meter consists of a choriambic kernel (−∪∪−) to which shorts and longs can be added. But ultimately, as the audience knew, Cassandra does not wed her captor Agamemnon, but is slain by his wife Clytemnestra (see pp. 43–44), so that by reason of its aeolic rhythm alone, her aria takes on a horrible irony.

The ionic meter (∪∪— —) is the "barbarian motif" of Greek tragedy. The music composed in this rhythm must have been emotive in the extreme, and consequently was regarded as enervating and oriental. Long sections of *Persians* are composed in ionics. The meter of Aeschylus's play is itself a sign of its exotic, Persian theme.

The rhythmic form is thus a kind of signal. The narrative parts of the parodos of *Agamemnon* (see pp. 39ff.) are delivered in dactylo-epitrite, a meter associated with the narrative genre of dithyramb. It consists of a combination of dactylic (—∪∪—∪∪—) and epitritic (—∪—) elements joined by ancipitia (x). When, in the central part of the parodos, the chorus sings a hymn to Zeus, the meter changes to simple trochaics (—∪—x). The change in meter calls attention to the new subject: the hymn, which recalls the poetry of worship, stands out. A number of meters are expressive of strong emotion, above all dochmiacs (x— —∪—), a meter especially appropriate to the panic felt by the Theban women in the parodos of *Seven against Thebes* (see p. 34).

After the Persian Wars the music of the dithyramb and later of the other dramatic genres was transformed. Whereas in the dithyrambs of Pindar, which were performed to the accompaniment of the flute, the words were of greater importance than the music, later, from ca. 450, the music became more important than the words. This development is most apparent in the plays of Euripides. The solo came into vogue, which was in effect program music for a single voice. The rolling thunder, the whistling of the wind, the rat-a-tat-tat of hail, the creaking of wheels, the sound of trumpets and other musical instruments, even the barking of dogs, the bleating of sheep, and the chirping of birds, were imitated, as Plato records in the *Republic* (397a 1–7). Sound and sound effects became increasingly rich. Startling changes in rhythm and in key became common. Compositions with frequently alternating rhythms (polymetry) superseded those with a more or less uniform rhythmic theme. The traditional arrangement, in which the choral song was divided into strophe and antistrophe, was gradually abandoned. Polymetric compositions could not easily be performed by a chorus, which as a group was incapable of realizing the various rhythmic changes in dance and song. Thus, in the late works of Euripides the actor's solo became more and more frequent.

The content of a song is often at variance with its form, with the pathos of its language, with its meter, music, or choreography, as, for example, when the description of a trivial occurrence is couched in elevated and complex lyricism.

We may single out Ion's "cleaning song," or "broom aria" (*Ion* 82–183). Ion appears after the prologue, which is spoken by Hermes. His first words—a genre picture of Delphi followed by a description, in highly poetic terms, of his duties, the cleaning of the temple and the shooing of the birds whose droppings defile it are delivered in recitative (82–111). He begins the "cleaning song" proper (112–43) by calling on his laurel broom in an elaborate address that recalls the prayers to divinities made in hymns. There follows a concluding song (144–83), in the course of which Ion tries, with menacing shouts and gestures, to drive away the birds that have taken residence in the sacred precinct.

The incongruity between lofty form and banal content in Ion's solo exemplifies the *palintonos harmonia* ('harmony of opposites') that characterizes the structure, action, and content of Euripides' late plays (see p. 117).

Chorus and Dramatic Action

People are predisposed to infer the general from the particular, the ideal from the material. In tragedy, too, this manner of reflection has its place. But to merit this place, it must recover in the tragic performance the material life that is lost in the deductive process. For if the two elements of poetry, the ideal and the material, do not act in union, they must do so *side by side*. Otherwise there can be no poetry. If the scales of a balance are not in perfect equipoise, it is only by *tilting* the pans that one can make them so.

Such is the function of the chorus in tragedy. The chorus is itself not an individual, but rather a general concept represented in material form, whose corporeal presence impinges deeply on the senses. It leaves the narrow circle of the action to meditate on past and future, on distant times and peoples, indeed on humanity itself, in order that it may derive great truths from human experience and pronounce the lessons of wisdom. Moreover, it does so with the vast might of the imagination, with a bold lyric freedom that scales, like a god, the heights of human affairs. Yet its lofty pronouncements are accompanied by all the material power of music, of melody, rhythm, and movement.

The chorus *purifies* the tragic poem by isolating these thoughts from the action, and thereby furnishes its meditation with poetic power, just as a sculptor or painter transforms the common necessity of clothing into drapery of extraordinary charm and beauty. (Friedrich von Schiller, "On the Use of the Chorus in Tragedy," preface to *The Bride of Messina*.)

Ancient tragedy differs from modern in yet another respect: the chorus. It must be understood as personified meditation on the action of the play, the embodiment of the poet's part in the performance as spokesman for all humanity. . . . The chorus is, in short, an idealized spectator. It mitigates what is shocking or moving in the performance by evincing for the actual spectator his own emotions in lyric, musical form and leading him up to the region of contemplation.

(August Wilhelm von Schlegel, *Lectures on Dramatic
Art and Literature*, Lecture 5.)

The influential views of Schiller and Schlegel, who saw
in the chorus of Greek tragedy "not an individual, but
rather a general concept," an "idealized spectator," a
device employed by the poet to express timeless truth and
wisdom, are at odds with the assessment of Aristotle,
who, in the eighteenth chapter of his *Poetics* (1456a 25–
27), praises Sophocles for giving the chorus a significant
role in the action of his plays.

What functions can in fact be assigned to the chorus of
Greek tragedy? A brief overview of the chorus in the
works of Aeschylus, Sophocles, and Euripides may bring
us closer to an answer.

In two of the extant tragedies of Aeschylus—*Eumenides*
and *Suppliants*—the chorus serves as a vehicle of the dramatic action. In *Eumenides* (see pp. 49ff.) the Erinyes
oppose Orestes, speaking out against him and advocating
their own cause at his trial before the Areopagus. The significance of the chorus in this play emerges from its lyric
dialogue with Athena (778ff.) following Orestes' acquittal.
In two pairs of odes the Erinyes give vent to their boundless
pain. Their intransigence and obstinacy, which Athena's
soothing words cannot mitigate, is underscored by structural correspondence: the second ode in each pair matches
the first exactly in content and metrical arrangement. In
this way the contrast between the choral parts, with their
uneasy lyric rhythms, and Athena's mollifications, which
she utters in ordinary, conversational iambic trimeter, is
made emphatic.

The daughters of Danaus, who form the chorus of *Suppliants* (see pp. 36ff.), are central to that play. At first the
chorus leader attempts to obtain asylum from Pelasgus for
herself and her sisters, as sole representative of their common cause. Once it has become apparent, however, that
she alone cannot win him over, the chorus enters in a

body and overwhelms the king with its urgent appeal. In this play, as in *Eumenides*, metrical form reinforces content and serves to characterize both parties. The passionate entreaties of Danaus's daughters, who threaten to take their own lives, are cast in agitated lyric rhythms, while the king, pondering his dilemma, vacillating, continues to speak in iambic trimeter. The same structure (the alternation between choral song and verse spoken by an actor, known as "epirrhematic composition") is found in *Seven against Thebes*, where Eteocles' placations, spoken in iambic trimeter, collide with the halting rhythms of the anxious chorus of Theban maidens (203ff.).

The Cassandra scene of *Agamemnon* (1072ff.) evinces the expressive potential of lyric verse, as opposed to dialogue (or recitative), and indeed is particularly striking in this respect. As Cassandra sings, the chorus leader, speaking for the chorus of old Argive men, complains in iambic trimeter of his inability to comprehend the seeress's words (1072–1113). Only when the fear inspired by Cassandra's presentiments has overcome the old men do they also begin to sing (1119ff.).

Another function of the chorus is evident in the parodos of *Agamemnon* (see pp. 39ff.). Although the old men of Argos know nothing of the beacon received by the watchman at the outset of the play, they are nevertheless disquieted about the fate of the Greek army. In their troubled state they reflect on the origins of the war. Through their contemplation of the past they widen the dimensions of the dramatic action. In their hymn to Zeus, which occupies the center of this long choral passage, they put forth the theological meditation that informs the entire trilogy, without overstepping the limits of their character or violating the logic of the dramatic action.

In Aeschylus's *Persians* the chorus has still another function. At no point do the Persian elders who form the chorus, though they give the play its title, serve as the vehicle of the action to the extent to which the choruses do in

Eumenides and *Suppliants*. Rather, it represents a distinctly Persian background and conveys to the Greek audience, in a "furioso of misery" (A. Lesky, *Die tragische Dichtung der Hellenen*, 3rd ed. [Göttingen, 1972] 84), something of the traumatic impact of Xerxes' devastating defeat.

In neither Sophocles nor Euripides do we find a chorus so involved in the action as those of Aeschylus's *Eumenides* and *Suppliants*. Aristotle drew attention to an essential characteristic of the Sophoclean chorus when he praised that poet for having his choruses take part in the dramatic action. In no extant tragedy of Sophocles can the chorus be said to advance the plot, and yet it does participate in dramatic events as a distinct "personage"; its utterances are to be understood as those of a minor character (see pp. 69–70 on *Antigone*). The chorus in Euripides is much less an independent personage than it is in Sophocles. A comparison of Aeschylus's *Suppliants* with the Euripidean play of the same title is instructive. The choruses in both tragedies consist of suppliants. In Aeschylus, however, the daughters of Danaus represent their own cause; in Euripides the chorus is represented first by Aethra and later by Theseus. The chorus in Euripides' play does little more than give the characters a reason to act. Even in *Bacchae*, in many respects an archaic play, the chorus, which consists of devotees of the god Dionysus, far from actively shaping the events of the play, serves rather as a background against which those events are projected.

The chorus, in sum, seems to have developed along the following lines. In Aeschylus it serves as a vehicle of the dramatic action, and in Sophocles becomes a distinct dramatis persona with a minor part in that action. The Euripidean chorus, by contrast, dismayed at what is happening around and in part because of it, no longer participates in the action but only sympathizes with the actors.

It was Agathon who, towards the end of the fifth century, took the next step. His choruses were isolated from

the dramatic action and delivered songs bearing no relation to what was represented on the stage. Such choral
songs, or *embolima* ('inserts') found their way, via Hellenistic drama, into Senecan tragedy, were later revived in the
form of the *reyen* ('choral songs') of German Baroque tragedy, which show Senecan influence, and finally were
reflected in the theoretical and practical work of Classi-
cism and Romanticism.

II

AESCHYLUS

Life and Works

Born at Eleusis in 525/4, Aeschylus belonged to one of the old aristocratic families of Attica, the so-called Eupatridae, or families with noble fathers. He presumably made his debut as a tragic poet in 499; he won his first victory in 484. He fought against the Persians at Marathon in 490 and again at Salamis in 480. In 476/5 he was invited by the tyrant Hieron I of Syracuse to stage *Women of Aetna* at the dramatic festival held on the occasion of the foundation of Aetna in Sicily. He returned to Sicily, again at the invitation of Hieron, to restage *Persians*, first performed at Athens in 472. It is not, however, clear from the sources whether Aeschylus in fact made two trips to Sicily within such a short period. If he made only one trip, his *Women of Aetna* would not have been performed in 476/5, but after 472 and thus some years after the foundation of Aetna. It was during a third (or second) stay in Sicily, at Gela in 456/5, that he died.

Such are the scanty facts about the life of Aeschylus that remain fairly certain once we have sifted through the largely anecdotal evidence. Seen against the background of Athenian political history, they take on greater significance. Aeschylus witnessed the formation of the Athenian democracy and the emergence of Athenian self-consciousness. He was fifteen in 510, when, after the murder of Hipparchus (a son of the tyrant Peisistratus) at the hands of the "tyrant-slayers" Harmodius and Aristogeiton (514), the Athenians put an end to the Peisistratid tyranny by expelling Hipparchus's brother Hippias. It was also at about this time that Cleisthenes passed his political reforms, thereby laying the foundations of democratic government in Athens. As a soldier Aeschylus had a hand in the greatest triumphs of the young democracy, the victory over the Persians at Marathon by land (490) and at Salamis by sea (480). He lived to see the transition to radical democracy effected by the legislation of Ephialtes in 462/1, which deprived the Areopagus, the old aristocratic council that had been preeminent especially since the Persian Wars, of its political influence and restricted its jurisdiction to cases of homicide.

Thus, two influences are paramount in Aeschylus's biography. He experienced the democratization of Athens. On the other hand, he was repeatedly drawn to the court of the tyrant Hieron of Syracuse. The court of the Sicilian tyrant fascinated the greatest poets of the day, and Aeschylus, like the choral poets Simonides, Pindar, and Bacchylides, succumbed to its allure.

For the Athenians of the year 405—that is, some fifty years after his death—Aeschylus was the poet of that glittering age in which the Athenian democracy came to assert its strength in the face of formidable enemies both within and without Attica. In *Frogs* (1021ff.) Aristophanes has Aeschylus characterize his tragedies as "full of Ares," that is, full of battle descriptions and the fury of war; the comic poet also puts into Aeschylus's mouth the claim that he encouraged the Athenians to emulate the ideal conduct that he represented on the stage. It is to this end, he explains, that his tragedies are clothed in lofty diction, in words endowed with an infectious, elemental force

(814ff.). Aristophanes is contrasting his own gloomy age, the final, hopeless phase of the Peloponnesian War, an age marked, like the plays of Euripides, by the achievements of the sophists, with one in which men were by nature pious, like Aeschylus himself, and still took the interests of the commonwealth to heart, an age in which everything, including the poetry, was better.

Aeschylus's reputation as the tragic poet par excellence in the eyes of the Athenians of 405 was not simply due to the fact that his plays continued to be restaged long after his death. Even in his own day Aeschylus was more successful in the tragic competition than any other poet. Although it presumably took him seven attempts, after his debut in 499, to win his first victory (484), thereafter he was probably victorious twelve times, that is, every time he took part in the dramatic competition.

If this reconstruction is correct, Aeschylus composed twenty tetralogies (80 plays) in his career as a tragic poet. Seven tragedies have come down to us under his name, some of which can be securely dated: *Persians* (472), *Seven against Thebes* (467), and the *Oresteia*, consisting of *Agamemnon, Choephori*, and *Eumenides* (458). The remaining two, *Suppliants* and *Prometheus Bound*, are more difficult to date. Owing to the dominant role played by its chorus, *Suppliants* was long regarded as the most archaic and consequently the earliest of Aeschylus's plays, but it can now be placed, on the basis of a papyrus find published in 1952, within the years 465–460; 463 seems the most plausible date. Finally, *Prometheus Bound* cannot have come from Aeschylus's pen, at least not in the form in which we have it: linguistic and stylistic criteria, its dramatic composition, and its thoroughly un-Aeschylean stage effects and theology all tell against its authenticity. The play may be the product of a later age, conceived as a counterpart to the genuine *Prometheus Unbound*, perhaps on the occasion of a restaging of the latter; or it may be that a *Prometheus Bound* originally composed by Aeschylus was rewritten to comply with the tastes of a later audience. What follows is an outline of the plot:

At the behest of Zeus, Prometheus, the benefactor of mankind, is nailed to a rock by Hephaestus with the help of his henchmen Cratus (Might) and Bia (Violence). In a long apologia delivered before the daughters of Oceanus (the chorus), who have come to learn the reason for his distress and to offer him their compassion, Prometheus lists the benefits that mortals have received from him (436ff.). Io now bursts onto the stage. She has been transformed into a cow and left to roam the earth: like Prometheus, she has Zeus to blame for her unhappiness (561ff.). Prometheus prophesies that Zeus will not put an end to Io's restless wandering until she reaches Egypt. In that land she will bear Zeus a son, Epaphus, whose descendant Heracles will one day liberate Prometheus from his suffering (669f.). Yet even Zeus's rule, Prometheus reveals, will be of limited duration, because the god, in union with a mortal woman, is destined to beget his own master. Because Prometheus refuses to give the divine messenger Hermes more precise information about Zeus's undoing (928ff.), Zeus causes him, along with the chorus, to sink beneath the earth amid a turmoil of the elements.

History as Myth: *Persians*

Persians, produced in 472 together with *Phineus, Glaucus*, and the concluding satyr play *Prometheus*, is the only extant Aeschylean work that is not part of a thematically unified trilogy. The play is our only complete example of several efforts in the first quarter of the fifth century to bring contemporary history onto the stage. Aeschylus had a precursor in Phrynichus, who in his *Capture of Miletus* (492?) and *Phoenician Women* (476) dramatized historical events of the recent past. Phrynichus's *Capture of Miletus* dealt with the end of the Ionian Revolt against the Persians (494), and *Phoenician Women* represented, like Aeschylus's *Persians*, the consequences of the Persian defeat at Salamis (480) from the perspective of the conquered. Insofar as the fragments allow us to reconstruct the action, *Phoenician Women* seems to have opened with the announcement of Xerxes' defeat by a Persian eunuch. The Phoenician women from Sidon who form the chorus (the Phoenicians supplied a major part of the Persian fleet) feel the agony of the catastrophe most keenly, for they must endure the loss of their husbands, brothers, and sons who fell at Salamis.

In his *Phoenician Women*, Phrynichus presumably did not exploit the dramatic potential inherent in the situation of an uncertain chorus anxiously awaiting news of the war, but instead concentrated on the reaction of the chorus, in a sequence of lamentations, to the report of the Persian defeat. Aeschylus's chorus, by contrast, must wait for tidings of the campaign in an atmosphere of slowly mounting tension. *Persians* falls into three lengthy sections. First, a mood of oppression is established in the entrance song (1–139) of the chorus, which consists of old Persians, the crown council of Xerxes, king of Persia. The old men show pride and confidence in the greatness of the Persian army, but they are also concerned about the fate of the armed forces tarrying in enemy territory. The chorus, which stands for the whole of Persia, vacillates between hope and fear, and its uncertainty is exacerbated by Atossa, Xerxes' mother, who has been disturbed by an ominous dream (176ff.). In the second section, this tension is abruptly dispelled when a messenger arrives to tell of the catastrophic defeat of the Persian army (249ff., esp. 302ff.). The nucleus of the play is the scene in which the ghost of Darius, Xerxes' father, is conjured up from the realm of the dead by the chorus. In what is in effect an addendum to the

messenger's speech, Darius explains to Atossa and the old
men why Xerxes has thus far been defeated, predicts the
catastrophe of the Persian land army at Plataea, and warns
them never again to take the field against the Greeks
(681ff.). In the third and last section, the defeated king
returns; his arrival has been much anticipated. Together
with the chorus, though without his retinue, without an
appropriate reception, even without meeting his eagerly
waiting mother, laments the downfall of Persian greatness.

As this sketch of the basic structure of *Persians* shows,
it was not Aeschylus's aim to stage a series of exciting
events so much as to ask how Persia, for all its imperial
might, could be brought to ruin. The play offers an explanation for Xerxes' failure. To do this, Aeschylus treated
contemporary history as myth, reworking material that
was known to the entire audience—the same historical
events had already been dramatized by Phrynichus—and
interpreting it in his own way. This method is best illustrated by the Darius scene (681–851), which is essential
to the interpretation of the play. The poet cleverly pre-
pares for the epiphany of the king by having Atossa ask
the chorus to raise the ghost of her husband from the
underworld (619–21), and in the choral song (*hymnos
klētikos*) that follows, the old men call on the deified
ruler to appear. The god-king is idealized as the ruler of
an earlier and better age, one who never led Persian sol-
diers to destruction on rash campaigns (653–56). The
chorus omits any mention of his failed campaign at Marathon in 490.

As god and ideal ruler, Darius accounts for Xerxes's mis-
fortune from a higher, absolutely valid standpoint, as it
were *ex cathedra*. He first puts the blame on an evil and
deceptive *daimōn*, or divine power (725), just as the messenger (354), Atossa (472, 724), and the chorus (515) had
done before him, before giving a fuller explanation (739–
52):

Alas, the fulfillment of the oracles came swiftly! It was at my son that Zeus hurled down the issue of those prophecies! I was sure that in due course the gods would bring these things to pass. Whenever one is too ambitious, god lends a hand. Now, it seems, a fount of ills has been found for all my loved ones. My son accomplished these things unwittingly, in the boldness of youth, who thought that he could check the flow of the sacred Hellespont, the divine current of the Bosporus, as one would chain a slave; who sought to alter its passage; who, by casting hammered fetters over it, made a huge path for a huge army. Though only mortal, he thought—on bad counsel— that he would overpower all the gods, even Poseidon. Was my son not mad? I am afraid that the wealth for which I toiled may now be plundered by the first comer.

Darius does not call into question the influence of the *daimōn*; he had once heard from an oracle of a disaster that would one day bring the Persians to ruin. But Xerxes alone is to blame for the fact that this calamity overtook his people so swiftly and unexpectedly. His ardent desire to measure up to his father and his thirst for action led Xerxes to heed the ill-advised promptings of his friends and undertake the expedition against Greece, for "whenever one is too ambitious, god lends a hand" (742). Xerxes was overzealous and transgressed the limits that had been set by the gods for the Persians, who had been told to exercise their power only on land. The crossing of the Bosporus, the attempt to subdue Poseidon, god of the sea, was an act of mortal presumption (*hybris*) and inevitably brought retribution in its train (745–50). Given this interpretation, two stanzas from the parodos take on new meaning: there the chorus emphasizes that from time eternal, the gods gave the Persians supremacy on land (101–5), while seafaring was not god-given, but acquired by learning (109–14).

By crossing the sea, Xerxes rendered himself liable to "treacherous god-sent delusion" (93) and was overcome by bewilderment (*atē*), from whose net there is no possibility of escape: the more Xerxes struggled, driven by *hybris*, the more entangled he became in this net.

Aeschylus has Darius expound a theodicy: the blame that mortals unreflectively attribute to the gods he places on mortals themselves. The mortal who, like Xerxes, purposes to subdue the gods is held accountable for his actions and incurs guilt; yet, as Darius intimates in his prophecy (800ff.), he can, through suffering, find his way to wisdom.

Seven against Thebes

Performed in 467 together with *Laius, Oedipus,* and the satyr play *Sphinx, Seven against Thebes* is the last play of a trilogy that traced the downfall of Laius, king of Thebes, and his descendants. *Laius* told the story of the king's death. Laius begets a son. Since an oracle of Apollo once admonished him to remain childless, foretelling that, if he did not, it was fated that he should perish at the hands of his child, the king has the babe exposed, and imagines that he has thwarted the oracle. But the servant charged with this task takes pity on the boy and gives it to a Corinthian shepherd. Many years later the king's fate catches up with him. At a crossing of three roads he is struck down by his son Oedipus. In *Oedipus* the son discovers the truth— that he has slain his father and married his mother. In despair he puts out his eyes and curses his sons Eteocles and Polyneices. Finally, in *Seven*, the brothers die at each other's hands; the curse is fulfilled. Such were, presumably, the broad lines of the trilogy, sketched on the basis of the myth. Further reconstruction is precluded by the limited comparative material available to us; the *Oresteia* is the only trilogy that could be adduced in support of such

a reconstruction (it is the only complete trilogy to survive), and it tells the story of only two generations.

The central scene of *Seven* is a sequence of seven pairs
of speeches in which Eteocles pits a Theban against each
of seven Argive attackers (375–676). This middle section
is preceded by the parodos (78–180) sung by the chorus of
Theban women, whose hysteria contrasts sharply with
the peremptory words of Eteocles (1–38, 181ff.). The seven
pairs of speeches are followed by the entreaties of the
chorus (677ff.), which seeks to dissuade Eteocles from his
decision, made in the final pair of speeches (631–76), to
take up arms against his brother. The last part of the tragedy (792ff.) is taken up with the Theban reaction to the
report of the double fratricide. This conclusion was
appended by a latter interpolator, who introduced the sisters Antigone and Ismene as well as a herald who issues a
decree banning the burial of Polyneices. The interpolator
was most likely making the end of Aeschylus's play conform with the beginning of Sophocles' *Antigone*—perhaps
when *Seven* was being restaged along with Sophocles' play.
The conclusion would then have served as a link between
the two plays. In the opening section of *Seven*, as in that of
Persians, an atmosphere of suspense is created; in the middle section the suspense is relieved; and in the final section there is a reaction to its relief.

Just as the interpretation of *Persians* hinges on its central scene, in which the ghost of Darius appears, so that of
Seven hinges on the seven pairs of speeches that make up
the central section of the play. Thebes is under siege. Eteocles tries to calm the chorus, which is close to panic, and
declares that he and six other men are going to defend the
seven gates of the city (282f.). Later, after a long choral passage in which the horrors of depredation are described in
lurid detail (287–368), Eteocles returns and is met by a
scout who tells him in seven speeches whom the Argives
are sending against each of the seven gates of Thebes. The
king answers each of the seven speeches in turn, matching

a Theban warrior with each Argive adversary. In one instance he has made his decision in advance; in another he makes it only after having heard the report of the scout. This process of selection is indicated by the tenses that Eteocles uses in naming the various defenders. In answer to the scout's first speech, Eteocles exclaims (in the future tense) that he will send out the Theban Melanippus against Tydeus, the attacker at the first gate. In his next three responses, however, he uses the past tense; he has decided in advance who will defend the second, third, and fourth gates. The defender of the fifth gate is sent off in the present tense, which leaves open the question whether the king's decision is spontaneous; those of the sixth and seventh gates are spontaneously chosen (in the future tense). It is therefore clear that Eteocles decides of his own free will to oppose his own brother Polyneices at the seventh gate. Once he has made this decision, he recognizes the significance of his father's curse and of the dreams that have been frightening him. He is not only the self-sacrificing defender of the homeland but also the son of Oedipus, consigned to destruction by his father's imprecation (653–55): "O maddened by divinity, loathed greatly by the gods, O much bewept, our family, that of Oedipus: alas, now indeed are my father's curses being brought to fulfillment!"

The theology that emerges from this interpretation of the seven pairs of speeches may be compared with the theodicy of *Persians:* Eteocles has been doomed by his father's curse, but just as Xerxes hastens the fulfillment of the oracle given to Darius by his own insolent actions, so Eteocles precipitates his own undoing by resolving to face his brother. The admonitions of the chorus, which pleads with him to change his mind, fall upon deaf ears. Whereas, however, in *Persians* Darius showed his countrymen how they might avoid disaster in the future by warning them never again to take the field against the Greeks, in *Seven* no such lesson is drawn: at no point is it suggested that suffering may bring a kind of saving knowledge. Every spectator knew all too well, as did the interpolator of the final scene, that the misfortunes of the Labdacids would not end with the deaths of Eteocles and Polyneices.

Suppliants

Suppliants, it is generally agreed, was the opening play of the Danaid trilogy. The reconstruction of the trilogy, despite the ingenious attempts of a number of scholars, must still be regarded as an unsolved problem. Unlike the Theban trilogy and the *Oresteia*, the Danaid trilogy did not trace the fate of two or three generations of a royal house; instead, it focused on the fifty Danaids, or daughters of Danaus. The plot of the extant play is simple. Pursued by their cousins, the sons of Aegyptus, who seek to marry them against their will, the maidens take flight and are granted asylum in Argos after a bitter confrontation with its king, Pelasgus. The threats of war leveled against the king by the Egyptian herald, who withdraws when Pelasgus appears with his Argive army, were made good in the second play, *Egyptians*. Pelasgus, it seems, was killed in the fighting; the daughters of Danaus were forced to marry their cousins but at their father's behest murdered their grooms on the night of their wedding.

One Danaid, Hypermnestra, fell in love with her groom and, disobeying her father, chose to spare him. It was probably in *Danaids*, the final play of the trilogy, that her story was told. A long fragment from the play contains part of Aphrodite's speech in praise of the cosmic power of love. The goddess, it has been argued, interceded on behalf of Hypermnestra when she was put on trial for filial disobedience. Thus father and daughter were reconciled in the end. The satyr play *Amymone* reflected the themes of the preceding tragedies, but here the tone was less serious. Amymone, another daughter of Danaus, was pursued by a satyr; she was rescued by Poseidon and became the god's mistress.

The structure of *Suppliants* differs from that of the plays hitherto discussed, in that the central scene (234–523), in which the chorus of maidens grapples with Pelasgus, is not followed by a reaction to that section, as in *Persians* and *Seven*, which close with reactions to the epiphany of Darius and to Eteocles' decision to oppose his brother, respectively. Instead, the Egyptian herald (825ff.), and, in the final scene, the second chorus of servants — which counters the maidens' song in praise of chaste Artemis (1030–33) with one in praise of Aphrodite (1034ff.) — adumbrate themes to be developed in the subsequent plays of the trilogy.

Because *Suppliants*, as the first member of the trilogy, is expositive, it is impossible to discern in it a theology such as emerges from *Persians*, which was not part of a thematically unified trilogy, or from *Seven*, which was the final play of such a trilogy. Similarly, because the play is open-ended, it is not clear why the Danaids do not want to marry their Egyptian cousins.

An examination of all the passages in which the Danaids speak of marriage reveals that they are not averse to marriage as such; it is only the forced union with the sons of Aegyptus that they reject. When Pelasgus asks them why they are fleeing from these men, they are vague and evasive (336, 390f.). In the first play Aeschylus lays the groundwork for the action of the second and third plays. Just what motivated the Danaids to spurn their cousins — several motives are mentioned (by the maidens themselves, Pelasgus, the herald, and the second chorus) — is a question that the poet presumably answered more definitively by the end of the trilogy.

Crucial to the interpretation of *Suppliants* is the long series of scenes in the central part of the play (234–523), in which Pelasgus must decide whether to grant asylum to the Danaids — the first decision scene in extant Greek tragedy. Pelasgus has to choose between two evils. If, on the one hand, he decides in favor of the Danaids, he faces war with the spurned suitors and jeopardizes Argos; if, on the other, he decides against the suppliants, he breaches his civic duty, violates Zeus Hikesios, champion of those in need of protection, and saddles the city with an unbearable defilement, since the Danaids have threatened to kill themselves at the altar where they have taken refuge. The king, who recognizes his dilemma (379f. and esp. 407–17), is indecisive. But the Danaids' threat of suicide forces him to decide: coercion is the central motif in this scene. He grants them asylum (478f.), thereby placing religious duty before the weal of the polis. Later the king can take consolation in the fact that he has avoided the wrath of the gods by deciding in favor of Zeus Hikesios.

The *Oresteia*

Aeschylus's *Oresteia* is the only trilogy that has come down to us in its entirety (*Proteus*, the satyr play with which the tetralogy ended, has not been preserved). We are able to see how the poet treated, within the frame of three thematically connected plays, the destiny of two heroic generations (Agamemnon and Orestes); the past, both recent and remote, of the house of Atreus; and difficult theological problems—the relationship between gods and mortals and that between human guilt and divine causality. Here is our one opportunity to study how he might set forth and solve all these problems within the unified structure of a trilogy.

The plot of the three plays can be summarized briefly. In *Agamemnon* the king returns from Troy and is struck down in his bathtub by his wife; in *Choephori* Agamemnon's son, Orestes, grown to manhood, takes revenge on his mother and her lover, Aegisthus; finally, in *Eumenides* Orestes, tormented by the Erinyes, the avenging goddesses, for having murdered his mother, is absolved from his blood guilt by an Athenian jury court set up especially for this purpose by Athena, the goddess of the city. At first this verdict only exacerbates the anger of the Erinyes, but Athena uses flattery to convince them to make their residence henceforth in Athens, transformed into Eumenides—kindly, beneficent goddesses.

Such is the action that unfolds in the course of the trilogy. That action is presented against a background of events not only of the recent past (the sacrifice of Iphigencia in Aulis at the hands of her father, Agamemnon, and the Trojan War), but also of the remote past (the terrible vengeance taken by Atreus, Agamemnon's father, on his brother Thyestes, when he invited Thyestes to a banquet on the pretense of a reconciliation and served him the flesh of his own sons, with the exception of little Aegisthus).

The structure of *Agamemnon* is marked by the tension between the stage action, the events of the past, and Agamemnon's anticipated return, which is the culmination of a series of increasingly exciting scenes in the first part of the play (1–781).

The prologue (1–39) is spoken by a watchman who has long been waiting for the beacon that is to signify the victory of the Greeks at Troy. Already there is an intimation that all is not well in his master's house (18f.). He paradoxically describes Clytemnestra as a woman with the heart and counsels of a man (11), and in his cryptic reference to circumstances in the palace (36–39) there is good reason to be apprehensive about Agamemnon's return.

The parodos is the longest continuous choral passage in extant Greek tragedy (40–257), a composition in which narrative and reflective sections are organically integrated. In this passage the chorus of old Argive men expounds, and tentatively interprets, the events that led to the Trojan War. The old men do not know, as the audience does, that the beacon has flashed, that the ten-year war is over, and that they can stop their anxious brooding at last. The passage begins with the origins of the war. Zeus, one of whose functions (as Zeus Xenios) is to punish those who violate the law of hospitality, once sent the sons of Atreus, Agamemnon and Menelaus, against Troy because Paris, the Trojan prince, had abused Menelaus's hospitality by running off with his host's wife, Helen. But the launching of the expedition was attended by an ambiguous omen. The refrain—"Sing a dirge, a dirge, but may the good prevail!"—that the chorus weaves into its narrative applies not only to the omen but also to the course of the whole trilogy. Two eagles, the chorus relates, struck down a pregnant hare. According to the interpretation of the seer Calchas, whose words are reported by the chorus in direct speech, the omen is propitious: the Greeks will take Troy and all its treasures. But the sign also has its gloomy side: Artemis has been angered by the eagles' feast and, the seer reflects, could send adverse winds and delay the Greek ships. Everyone in the audience knows where the narrative is leading. Agamemnon will propitiate the goddess by sacrificing his daughter Iphigeneia.

The old Argives interrupt their narrative just before its culmination to sing a hymn to Zeus (160–83). The shift from narrative to prayer comes as a surprise and is marked by a change of rhythm: majestic dactyls are replaced by modest trochees. The audience's attention is directed to what follows by the rhythmical—that is, the musical— signal.

The third and concluding strophe (176–83) contains the theological doctrine that is crucial for the interpretation not only of the trilogy but also of the entire Aeschylean corpus:

Zeus, who set mortals on the path to understanding, who ordained that "learning by suffering" should have the force of law. The toil that reminds one of his woes trickles before his heart instead of sleep. Wisdom comes even to the unwilling. Potent, I suppose, is the favor of divinities seated on their awesome bench.

The rule of Zeus is explained as a severe schooling of mortals, who are to follow the doctrine "learning by suffering" (*pathei mathos*) and thus arrive at "understanding" (*sōphronein*). Understanding comes even to those who close their minds to it. The rule of the supreme god is marked by violence, compulsion, and severity (*bia*) but also by benevolence (*charis*). For ultimately mortals do not see themselves at the mercy of arbitrary and unfathomable powers, but can, through suffering, attain understanding of both their own actions and the divine law that governs the universe.

Having expounded this theodicy, the chorus returns to its narration of the events that led to the Trojan War. At first the transition from the hymn back to the narrative is not reflected in the meter. Verses 184–91 form the antistrophe that corresponds metrically to the final strophe of the hymn (176–83). This metrical overlap clearly indicates that the subsequent description of the events at Aulis is to be interpreted in the light of the theodicy developed in the hymn. Just as Calchas had feared, there is no favorable wind to convey the ships. He urges a ghastly remedy: that the angry Artemis be propitiated by the sacrifice of Iphigeneia. Like Pelasgus in *Suppliants*, Agamemnon finds himself compelled to make a tragic decision. No matter what he decides, he must saddle himself with guilt (206–17).

It is grievous ruin for me not to obey, grievous ruin to slay my child, the delight of my house, polluting a father's hands with streams of a slaughtered maiden's blood by the altar. Which of these alternatives is free from ill? How am I to become a deserter of my ships, failing my allies? It is lawful for them to desire, with passion that overreaches passion, a sacrifice, maidenly blood, to calm the winds. May it turn out well!

Like Eteocles in *Seven against Thebes,* Agamemnon is guilty because an internal impulse drives him to choose the death of his own kin.

The chorus now tells of the preparations for the sacrifice of Iphigeneia. It makes her father's cruelty painfully obvious, but stops short of describing the slaughter itself to repeat the central idea of the parodos: may justice accord understanding to those who have suffered (250f.).

The action now resumes from the point at which it left off in the prologue. Agamemnon will return, as the watchman anticipates, but not until toward the end of the second stasimon. In the first of the two intervening episodes (258–354) Clytemnestra tells the old men about the beacon. They interrogate her and seem convinced that Troy has fallen. In the second (489–680) a messenger announces that Agamemnon will arrive shortly.

The suspense created in the prologue and parodos is further intensified in these two episodes as the shadow of guilt and atonement is cast over the joy of victory. Clytemnestra wishes (320ff.) that in their hour of victory the Greeks not give way to passion and commit atrocities against the Trojans. Anyone familiar with Homer knows that her wish cannot be granted. For their offenses against the vanquished inhabitants of Troy, both divine and mortal, the Greeks must suffer the retribution of the gods.

In the first stasimon (355–488) the chorus moves from jubilation to anxiety as it reflects that those whose victory has been tainted by excessive bloodshed cannot escape divine retribution. In the herald's speech there is still a suggestion of the fine difference between victory and defeat, success and disaster. Having naively hailed his native land, he tells of the storm that afflicted the Greek fleet on its return journey, sparing only the commander of the expedition—for a worse fate, as the audience knows. That fate is intimated in the choral song (second stasimon) immediately following the herald's report (681–781). The old men reflect on the guilt of Paris, which led to the fall of Troy, then on the theological principle at work in this example: the gods have willed that mortals be punished for their crimes. The exaction of punishment, however, becomes itself a crime. What the gods have willed, then, is a cycle of crime and guilt. In effect, one crime engenders another.

Agamemnon now enters and is met by Clytemnestra. His homecoming, which has been anticipated from various perspectives, is the turning point of the play and a masterpiece of Aeschylean characterization and dramatic technique. Clytemnestra does not greet her husband. Instead she delivers a kind of apologia, addressed at first to the chorus, in which she tells at some length how she has despaired during his absence (855–76). Turning at last to Agamemnon, she justifies the absence of Orestes. Then with extravagant flattery she bids him enter the palace trampling delicate purple tapestries. He scruples to accept honors that, as he himself recognizes, belong to the gods. But Clytemnestra is able to persuade him that this display is due to him as victor, and at last he succumbs. Ignorant of her treachery, he blindly treads on the blood-red embroideries to his death.

The blindness of Agamemnon contrasts sharply with the insight of Cassandra, the seeress whom he took as his share of the Trojan booty. Cowering silently in his chariot, she looks on as the king is lured into the palace. Three times Clytemnestra bids Cassandra follow her into the house, and three times she receives no answer (1035–68). If in the previous episode Agamemnon succumbed to the flattery of Clytemnestra, the captive prophetess cannot be moved. Clytemnestra gives up and returns to the palace. Only now does Cassandra speak. She cries out as one lamenting the dead and in a series of visions sees the crimes of the house (1072–1177): first the banquet of Thyestes, at which Atreus served his brother the flesh of his own children, and then the murder of Atreus's son Agamemnon. Agamemnon, entangled in a net, will be struck down by Clytemnestra as he bathes. Thus Cassandra pro-

vides the historical frame within which the murder of Agamemnon must be seen. The root of this gruesome event is
the curse on the house of Atreus (1090ff.). The house of
the sons of Atreus—"house" in the sense both of "family"
and "palace"—engenders new crimes through old ones,
as the chorus has already said in a more general context.
Cassandra now (1178ff.) interprets for the chorus what she
has seen in ordinary spoken iambics, a much quieter
meter than the agitated dochmiacs in which she described
her visions, referring explicitly to the curse on the house
of Atreus before stepping into the palace voluntarily and
in complete certainty of her imminent death.

The chief function of the Cassandra scene is to antici-
pate an offstage event, the murder of Agamemnon. The
passage in which she describes her visions is composed in
lyric dochmiacs, a meter well suited to her highly excited
mood. It was Aeschylus's bold innovation to replace the
conventional messenger's report, in which events that cannot be represented onstage are expounded in detail, with
Cassandra's prophetic vision of the murder of Agamemnon. Cassandra's prophecy represents the crystallization
point of the play and of the entire trilogy, the point at
which the intimations that were given in the prologue and
in the herald's report, as well as the fears and meditations
of the chorus, harden into gruesome certainty. Agamemnon's murder is now seen as only one in a series of ineluct-
able disasters that have befallen the house of Atreus as a
result of the operation of divine retribution.

Both the third episode, in which Agamemnon returns,
and the fourth, in which Cassandra describes her visions,
must have involved a remarkable combination of stage
background, stage properties, convention, innovation,
rhythm, music, dance, language, theology, and dramatic
action. The stage background, Atreus's house, takes on terrible significance when Cassandra tells of the crimes to
which it has been, or soon will be, witness. The purple tapestries on which Agamemnon steps after he has yielded to

Clytemnestra's flattery betoken his undoing. He treads them to his destruction, incurring at the same time the guilt of one who has offended the gods. The space between Clytemnestra and Agamemnon gives expression to their estrangement. In this episode Aeschylus makes use of the third actor, who was introduced by Sophocles, but has the actor playing the part of Cassandra remain silent until the next episode, with great effect.

The suspense reaches its highest pitch after Cassandra has gone into the palace and is horribly dispelled when Agamemnon's death screams are heard from within (1343, 1345). At this point the chorus takes counsel, with each of the twelve members of the chorus offering his opinion. Then the doors of the palace are thrown open, Clytemnestra appears, and the corpses of Agamemnon and Cassandra are seen on the *ekkyklēma*. On this "special stage" the interior scene is rolled out as a tableau. Clytemnestra approaches the chorus. Without remorse, and thus quite in character (10f.), she discloses what moved her to the deed: Iphigeneia's sacrifice at Aulis and Agamemnon's affairs with the daughter of Chryses at Troy and with Cassandra, whom he dared to bring into her house. When the chorus makes reference to the guiding principle of Aeschylean theology, "the doer must suffer" (1564), her self-confidence is shaken. She maintains that the responsibility for the murder of Agamemnon lies not with her but with a divine force that has encumbered the house of Atreus; she is merely the instrument of this force; with it she will make a pact, one of the terms of which will be that her husband's death will be the last link in the chain of crime and retribution.

In the final scene (1577ff.) the chorus encounters Aegisthus, who boasts that he has taken vengeance on Atreus's son Agamemnon. The outraged Argive elders are about to assail Aegisthus when Clytemnestra intervenes to prevent them from coming to blows. When the chorus reminds Aegisthus that Orestes may return to avenge the slaying of his father (1667), a link is established between *Agamemnon* and *Choephori*, the second play of the trilogy, the leading motif of which has already been announced by the chorus: "the doer must suffer" (1564).

In structure *Choephori*, the second play of the *Oresteia*, resembles *Agamemnon*. At its center is Orestes' murder of his mother. In an atmosphere of mounting suspense, the act of vengeance is conceived (1–651), carried out (652–972), and followed by the perpetrator's collapse (973–1076). The last part in effect links *Choephori* to *Eumenides*, the final play in the trilogy. After the matricide Orestes flees, pursued, at least in his troubled mind, by the Erinyes.

In *Choephori* are found motifs of great significance for the development of Greek drama, Euripidean tragedy and New Comedy in particular. Orestes, accompanied by his friend Pylades, has laid as a votive offering a lock of hair on Agamemnon's tomb. At the approach of the chorus they stand aside so as not to be seen. A train of captive Trojan women enters in attendance of Electra, who is visiting the tomb at the behest of Clytemnestra. The latter, terrified by a ghastly dream, has commissioned Electra to offer propitiatory libations to her father's ghost (hence the title of the play, which means "libation bearers"). This "eavesdropping scene" (22–83), which later, in New Comedy, became especially popular, is followed by the recognition of brother and sister (*anagnōrisis* or *anagnōrismos*) by means of tokens (*anagnōrismata*) that confirm Orestes' identity. Electra discovers Orestes' lock and concludes that it can only have been sent by Orestes. The grounds for her conviction are two: only Orestes would have dared, in the midst of such great enemies, to make an offering at the tomb of her father; the lock, moreover, resembles her own hair. When she discovers the footprints of Orestes and Pylades and it turns out that Orestes' footprint matches that of her own foot, she is certain. At this point Orestes emerges from his hiding place, tells her who he is, and shows her as final proof his garment, which she herself had woven.

In the central part of the play (652–972) Clytemnestra and Aegisthus are undone by an intrigue (*mēchanēma*). Whereas in *Agamemnon* the plot is kept secret until the moment of its execution, in *Choephori* it is contrived onstage. In order to gain entrance into the palace, Orestes, in the guise of a stranger passing through town, is to convey the tidings of his own death. But Aegisthus is not at home, and Clytemnestra sends Orestes' old nurse to fetch him and his bodyguard. Consequently the action is retarded and the suspense heightened. The chorus, which has taken the side of Orestes and Electra, intervenes to keep the plan from failing. Hinting that Orestes is not in fact dead, it instructs the nurse to tell Aegisthus to come alone, without his bodyguard. Aeschylus's treatment of the anagnōrismos and intrigue in *Choephori* should be compared with that of Sophocles and Euripides in their versions of the same material (see pp. 79ff.).

Pivotal for the interpretation of *Choephori* is the *kommos* (306–478), an antiphonal song or lyric dialogue between Orestes, Electra, and the chorus at Agamemnon's tomb. There is no consensus on the significance of this lyric composition. The discussion revolves around the question whether Orestes arrives at the decision to kill his mother in the kommos—that is, whether we can see in the kommos a situation in which a tragic decision is made, comparable to that of Pelasgus in *Suppliants*—or whether Orestes has already made up his mind to kill his mother before the kommos, and if this is the case, what purpose this long passage serves within the context of the play.

It emerges plainly from what Orestes says before the kommos that he is firmly resolved to kill his mother from the beginning. Apollo has given him the unequivocal command to carry out the deed and threatens him with dreadful torments should he disobey (269ff.). Orestes even says

that his own wishes are in accord with the god's oracle
(299ff.). He wishes to avenge his father's murder and,
being loath to lead the undignified life of an exile, to
recover the inheritance and rule of Argos that are his birthright. These personal motives are legitimized by the divine
command. So it is wrong to suppose that Orestes does not
make up his mind to obey Apollo's command until the
kommos, that he does not become a perpetrator acting on
his own impulses, and not merely an instrument of the
god, until then. For in fact he has accepted the divine command from the beginning. This interpretation finds additional support in 899ff. When Orestes is about to strike
down his mother, she bares her breast to arouse his pity.
He wavers, turning to Pylades in despair, who at this decisive moment speaks his only lines in the play. He reminds
his friend of Apollo's oracle and thus urges him to carry
out the deed. The words of Pylades, who is silent else-
where in the play, would be less effective were they not
spoken at a moment of crisis, when Orestes, temporarily
daunted, needs to be reminded of his resolve and steeled to
its execution.

An analysis of the structure of the kommos may shed
some light on its meaning. The passage can be divided
into three sections. In each section a change in structure
reflects a change in theme. The first section (306–422)
exhibits the following sequence, which occurs four times:
chorus (reciting in marching anapaests), Orestes (singing
a strophe), chorus (singing a strophe in the first and third
sequences, and in the third and fourth an antistrophe
responding to the strophe it sang in the first and second),
Electra (singing an antistrophe, responding to Orestes'
strophe). The leading motif is certainly the lamentation of
Agamemnon by Orestes and Electra (321, 335). Lamentation, however, is not the only theme. The chorus begins by
citing an ancient saying that recalls the words of the
chorus in *Agamemnon:* "The doer must suffer" (313–14;
cf. *Agamemnon* 1564). This saying implies an act of ven-

geance. Indeed, the function of the chorus in this section is to keep Orestes and Electra from lapsing into abstract reflection (e.g., 372–79) and so from losing sight of the act of vengeance which justice demands (e.g., 324–31, 340–44, 385–91).

In the second section of the kommos (423–55) the arrangement of parts is altered to mark a new theme: the dishonor suffered by Agamemnon and Electra at the hands of Clytemnestra. Agamemnon, Orestes learns, was buried without due lamentation, his corpse mutilated, and Electra has been virtually imprisoned in her palace chamber.

In the third and final section (456–78), which is also marked by a new arrangement of parts, Orestes, Electra, and the chorus call on Agamemnon's ghost and implore the assistance of the chthonic gods.

The kommos, then, gives lyric expression to the grievances that Orestes has already put forward against his father's killers (cf. esp. 300–301): Agamemnon's suffering and his children's loss of honor. These grievances, which he merely touched on just before the kommos, are not only illustrated by the chorus's reference to the savage mutilation of Agamemnon's corpse and Electra's description of her own maltreatment, but are shown to be justifiable grounds for vengeance, quite apart from Apollo's oracle, which is not even mentioned in the kommos. In this lyric passage Orestes, Electra, and the chorus prepare the audience emotionally, as it were, for the impending matricide by repeatedly referring to Clytemnestra as the authoress of their woes.

The structure of *Eumenides* is also threefold. The first part (1–234) is set at Delphi. Orestes, hounded by the Erinyes, has sought refuge in the temple of Apollo. Apollo has sent him to Athens, where he is to be tried for the murder of his mother and, Apollo promises, acquitted by a jury court established especially for this purpose. Roused by the ghost of Clytemnestra, the chorus of Erinyes leaves the orchestra in pursuit of Orestes and then re-enters to indicate a change of scene. Now on the Acropolis of Athens, the goddesses surround Orestes, who in suppli- cation clasps the wooden statue of Athena. The second part (235–777), which includes the trial scene, takes place on the Acropolis (the trial scene may take place on the Are- opagus). In the third and final part (778–1047) the Erinyes, who have been foaming with rage over their defeat, are transformed into beneficent, "well-meaning" goddesses and are given a new home at Athens.

Eumenides, especially in its prologue and parodos, is rich in stage effects that can, at least in part, be recon- structed on the basis of the text. The opening lines of the play are spoken by the Pythia, the priestess of Apollo at Delphi. The reverent words with which she invokes the god contrast sharply with the ending of *Choephori,* where Orestes left the stage hounded by the Erinyes. The priest- ess enters the temple through the central stage door (after 33) and immediately thereafter emerges from the shrine horror-stricken, staggering, indeed on all fours (37). A young man, recognizably a suppliant, sits holding a bloody sword at the *omphalos* ('navel'), a stone in the temple of Apollo at Delphi that marks the center of the earth. He is surrounded by snoring female creatures of frightening aspect.

Enter Apollo, Orestes, and (perhaps) Hermes. Apollo bids the young man depart for Athens under Hermes' pro- tection (64–93). The stage is vacant. Suddenly Clytemnes- tra's offstage voice is heard. It is her ghost rousing the Erinyes from their sleep (94–116). They are heard whining and moaning, muttering the commands of huntsmen in pursuit of quarry, dreaming aloud (117–39). Once awake, they emerge from the door one by one, loudly deploring the unspeakable dishonor that they, divinities from time immemorial, have suffered at the hands of the young god Apollo (140–78). Apollo himself appears and drives the hideous creatures from his sacred precinct (179–234). The heated words that they have with Apollo before they part anticipates their altercation with him at the trial. The Erinyes congregate to pick up Orestes' scent and quit the orchestra. Apollo leaves for Athens, where he will defend Orestes. The stage is again vacant. The scene changes to the Acropolis at Athens.

This reconstruction of the stage action, which is hotly disputed in the critical literature, has the advantage of creating an atmosphere of heightened suspense. *Choephori* ends with Orestes' vision of the Erinyes. The goddesses of vengeance whom the priestess describes are, however, visible beings. Being familiar with the conventions of the Attic stage, the audience would have assumed that the priestess was giving a kind of "messenger's report" in which something is described that the spectators are not allowed to see. After the entrance of Apollo and Orestes — an insertion that retards the action — the suspense is brought to an even higher pitch: hitherto unheard and unseen, the Erinyes are roused by Clytemnestra's ghost, begin their whining, and then, climactically, enter one after another, not onto the orchestra via the side entrances (*eisodoi*), but onto the stage through the central door of the stage building.

The conflict between the young and old gods, which first erupted when the Erinyes were driven from the Delphic shrine, culminates in the trial before the jury of Attic citizens under Athena's chairmanship, to whose judgment both parties promise to submit.

The arguments put forward in the trial scene, above all those of the defense, may seem strangely irrelevant and exaggerated to the modern reader, given that this scene is supposed to resolve the conflicts of the entire trilogy. In the trial scene Aeschylus certainly catered to the taste of his audience, which took pleasure in such quibbling contests, as similar scenes from tragedy and especially comedy show. It is not, however, the argumentation that is essential here, but rather the fact that the disastrous cycle of vengeance, the principle of the vendetta embodied by the Erinyes, is abolished by due process of law. Orestes is acquitted only by a parity of votes, one of which is cast by the goddess Athena as president of the court (she had stipulated that in the event of a parity of votes the accused would be acquitted). In the judgment of his fellow mortals, however, Orestes would have been found guilty: it is only Athena's vote that exonerates him.

The Erinyes, who as a result of their defeat feel divested of their traditional function, threaten to visit a blight upon Attica. Eventually, after a bitter struggle, the goddess is able to persuade them to give up their wrath by promising them divine honors as Eumenides. Their former function is not to be abolished completely, but neutralized, so to speak, in a new legal order. For, as the Erinyes themselves say before the beginning of the trial, "there are times when fear is a blessing" (517).

In the exodos the Eumenides are escorted in a solemn procession to their new home. Thus, the wish expressed in the second half of the refrain that runs through the parodos of *Agamemnon*—"Sing a dirge, a dirge, but may the good prevail!"—is fulfilled at the end of the trilogy. In the end, the good does prevail—but only after much suffering.

Politics and Aeschylean Tragedy

That Greek comedy abounds in allusions to contemporary political life, and that, in particular, it satirizes prominent political figures, is obvious, even if the function of these allusions is highly controversial. By contrast, the political background of Greek tragedy—that is, whether or to what extent politics should figure in the interpretation of the genre—is open to debate. Even less certain is the function of topical allusions in tragedy.

Much of the controversy has centered on Aeschylus. *Persians*, a play that brought recent history onto the Attic stage, is a case in point. A central motif in the play is the

praise of Athens as the leading power in Greece (230ff.).
Yet this distinction was patently anachronistic. Everyone
was well aware that Sparta had led the Greek resistance
against Persia. In particular, the messenger's account of
the battle of Salamis (353ff.) becomes in effect a panegyric
of Athens as the defender of Greek freedom against the
Persian invader. The play flattered the Athenian spectators, who were likely to have taken part in the battle, by
idealizing their achievements. The elevated form of the
tragic performance and the festive setting of the Great
Dionysia contributed to this idealization. Persians thus
heightened the self-esteem of the young democracy and
made emphatic Athens's claim to hegemony in the presence of the allies.

In view of the fact that Persians was performed shortly
before the ostracism of Themistocles, the hero of Salamis,
some have taken the messenger's report as evidence for
the poet's involvement in contemporary politics. Was the
play written, it is asked, in part to promote Themistocles'
cause? Although he is nowhere mentioned by name, few
in the audience will have missed the reference to the ruse
that was his brainchild (355ff.): the messenger tells how
the Athenian commander lured the Persians into the fateful battle by sending them the false report that the Greeks
would take flight during the night. Yet the prominence of
the battle at Salamis in the play is not in itself reason
enough to suppose that the poet was siding with Themistocles. In the messenger's description of the battle Aeschylus highlighted an event that made every Athenian proud
and showed how the city, unified and free from faction,
was able to ward off the Persian threat. The poet was making a plea for Athenian unity. Just as, more than fifty years
later and during a much more critical period for Athens in
both domestic and foreign affairs, the comic poet Aristophanes held up to his audience the Greek victory over the
Persians as an example to be emulated, the reward of internal concord and resolution in the face of the city's ene-

mies, so Aeschylus draws a picture of a harmonious past at
a time when it seemed that the consensus forged during
the Persian Wars was in danger of breaking apart.

Eumenides, which was staged four years after the
reforms of Ephialtes, also calls for political concord. Ephialtes, a champion of the radical democracy, had in 462/1
carried a motion for constitutional reform as a result of
which the powers of the old aristocratic council, the Areopagus (made up of all those who had held an archonship)
were curtailed: the council was deprived of any political
powers it may have had, retaining only the right to try cap-
ital cases and to oversee certain religious matters. Henceforth political power could be exercised by the popular
assembly (*ekklēsia*), council (*boulē*), and popular courts
(*Hēliaia* or *dikastēria*) without interference on the part of
the Areopagus. In *Eumenides* the goddess of the city, Athena, founds the council of the Areopagus and simply
assigns to it the authority which, roughly speaking, it had
after the reforms of Ephialtes: jurisdiction in murder cases.
A contemporary political event is thus relocated in mythical time. It is mythologized in the form of an *aition* (an
account of the origin of a phenomenon), as if this constitutional change had taken place in the days of Orestes, and
legitimated by the goddess Athena. If Aeschylus affirmed
the democratic reform, he also made a concession to its
opponents. The Areopagus council is constituted by divinity and thus accorded an extraordinary position, while its
prestige remains untainted. *Eumenides*, like *Persians*,
calls for rapprochement.

The ideal of harmony within the polis is a recurrent
theme in *Eumenides*. As the chorus leaves the stage in the
exodos, it prays for the welfare of the city in imploring
tones (976–87): "And, I pray, may faction, insatiate of ills,
not raise a din in this city. And may the dust in its wrath
not drink the dark blood of the citizens and devour the
penalties of murder in return for murder that bewilder a
city to its ruin. Rather may each give the other joy by

thinking of the common good, and hate with one mind: for among mortals this is a remedy for many things." In the new order, political differences are to be settled not by brute force, but by the power of Peitho, the personification of persuasive speech, with whose help Athena induced the Erinyes to give up their wrath against Athens (cf. 971f).

Aeschylean tragedy, as *Persians* and *Eumenides* well illustrate, was inspired with patriotic feeling. The elevated form of the genre lent splendor to contemporary events, which were represented either directly, as in *Persians*, or indirectly through a mythical *aition*, as in *Eumenides*. These plays heightened the self-consciousness of the citizens of Athens who had taken part in those events. The splendor of the city's achievements, filtered through and intensified by the poetry and pageantry of tragedy, reflected well on every member of the audience.

III

SOPHOCLES

Life and Works

Sophocles (497/6–406/5) was younger than Aeschylus by a generation: he was only a young man when Athens was already well on its way to becoming master of the Aegean. At sixteen he is said to have led the chorus that chanted the song celebrating the Athenian victory at Salamis. His life was infused with religion, cult, politics, poetry, with Athens and the Athenian democracy to a degree unmatched by any other dramatic poet. In 443/2 he held the office of *hellanotamias* ('treasurer of the Greeks'), and so was one of the ten leading men who managed the coffers of the Delian League. During the Samian War (441–439) he was *stratēgos* ('general') together with Pericles, to whose narrow circle he belonged. He occupied the same office again in 428, during the so-called Archidamian War (431–421), the first phase of the Peloponnesian War. In 413/2, when, after the catastrophic defeat of the Athenian expedition in Sicily, for which the radical democracy was held responsible, it was decided to restrict the powers of the democratic government, Sophocles was chosen to serve on a board of ten *probouloi*, or commissioners charged with supervising the legislative agenda of the council (*boulē*).

Sophocles also held religious office: he was a priest of the hero Halon and played a decisive role in the introduction of the cult of Asclepius from Epidauros to Athens (420). After his death he was honored as a hero with the title Dexion.

In his last work, the posthumously staged *Oedipus at Colonus*, Sophocles, who, unlike Aeschylus and Euripides, never left Athens, gave expression to his love for, and pride in, the land that was his home (668–719):

> Stranger, you have come to earth's finest abodes in this land of fine horses, to white Colonus, where the clear-voiced nightingale most often comes to warble deep in the covert of verdant glens, haunting the wine-dark ivy and the god's inviolate foliage that abounds in fruit, sheltered from the sun and the gusts of all storms, where the reveler Dionysus forever roams in the company of his divine nurses.
>
> And, sustained by the dew of heaven, the narcissus, crown of Demeter and Persephone from time past, blooms day by day with fair clusters, and the crocus with golden splendor. And the sleepless springs that feed the streams of Cephisus never dwindle, but every day the river reaches the plains, giving quick increase with the pure water of the broadly swelling earth. The choirs of the Muses do not shun this place, nor again does Aphrodite of the golden rein.
>
> And there is a tree that flourishes mightily in this land, invincible and self-renewing, such as I have heard has never sprouted either on Asian soil or on the great Dorian island of Pelops, a terror to enemy spears: the tree that bears the child-nourishing, shimmering olive. No commander, young or old, will with his hand ravage and destroy it, for the ever watchful eye of Zeus, protector of the sacred olives, gazes upon it, and Athena of the gleaming eyes.
>
> I have another word of praise to say, most mighty for this our mother city, a gift of the great god, a glory most great of fine horses, fine foals, a fine sea. O son

of Cronus, you seated Athens on this throne of glory,
lord Poseidon, when you invented the bit that tames
horses first in the streets of Colonus. And the well-
rowing oar, apt to Athenian hands, leaps amazingly
on the sea, a follower of the Nereids with their fifty
pairs of feet.

In the first strophic pair (strophe and antistrophe) the elders of the Attic deme Colonus, who form the chorus,
laud their birthplace (where Sophocles too was born); in
the second pair they sing of Athens, their mother city,
which enjoys the protection of Zeus, Athena, and Poseidon. Athena and Poseidon are both praised for having
made the city great, at a time (ca. 407/6) when a once
mighty Athens was perilously close to being shattered not
only from without, by the Spartans and their allies, but
also from within, by internal discord. Athena was the goddess of the democracy, and her statue was worshipped in
Pericles' Parthenon; Poseidon was the god of the aristocracy in his manifestation as Lord of Horses and yet, as god
of the sea and of seafaring, also a democratic divinity,
whose place of worship on the Acropolis was in the Erech-
theum, a temple erected by the aristocratic opposition.
Just as Aeschylus had done in *Eumenides*, a play written
during the first great internal crisis of the young democracy, Sophocles in *Oedipus at Colonus* drew an idealized
picture of a harmonious society in which the aristocracy
and the people jointly shouldered responsibility for an
Athens that was under the protection of the gods.

As a competitor at the dramatic festival Sophocles was
exceptionally successful. His first tetralogy in 468 also
brought him his first victory, and he continued to be successful in the years that followed. He was victorious with
eighteen of his thirty tetralogies; he never came in third,
that is, last.

Of the seven tragedies that have come down to us, only

two can be securely dated: *Philoctetes* (409) and *Oedipus at Colonus* (staged posthumously in 401, composed ca. 407/6). It is possible to deduce the date of *Antigone* from Sophocles' biography: Aristophanes of Byzantium (see p. 5) reports in his hypothesis that Sophocles was elected general, on the strength of the success of *Antigone*, during the Samian War (441–439). In view of the unreliable nature of the ancient biographies (see especially p. 86 on Euripides) we should not take this statement literally; that the two facts—the performance of *Antigone* and Sophocles' generalship—were coincident probably induced the biographer to assume a causal relationship between them. Consequently 440 is a plausible date for its performance.

All the same, a relative chronology can be established for the remaining plays on the basis of an analysis of their form and content. The characterization of Electra in the play that bears her name speaks for a date very close to that of *Philoctetes*, perhaps in the period 414–411. If this approximate date is correct, Sophocles' *Electra* was the "answer" to the Euripidean version of the same material; Euripides, for his part, offered a rejoinder to Sophocles' *Electra* in his *Orestes* (408). In the case of *Oedipus the King*, the *terminus post quem* of 429, hitherto generally accepted, has now been shown to be erroneous. The description of the pestilence in the prologue is not a reflection of the great plague at Athens but a well-known literary motif as old as Homer's *Iliad*; its function in *Oedipus the King* is simply to show how much the whole of the king's domain is made to suffer for his errors of ignorance. Plausible dates, as the studies of C. W. Müller have shown, are 436, 434, or 433. *Ajax* and *Trachinian Women* belong to an earlier period, the fifties or early forties, as is clear from similarities in their form and content. T. B. L. Webster has described the structure shared by these two tragedies as a "diptych," because they fall into halves without forfeiting their dramatic unity.

The Hero and His Environment:
Ajax — Trachinian Women

Ajax and *Trachinian Women* are similar in structure (both are "diptychs") and in substance. The focal point of both plays is a man of superhuman ability, a hero or demigod on whom the thinking and actions of others depend.

Sophocles took the material for his *Ajax* from the Trojan Cycle. The story is told in the epitomes of two lost epics, the *Aethiopis* and *Little Iliad*. After the death of Achilles a quarrel erupts over the fallen hero's armor. The two commanders of the Greek army, Agamemnon and Menelaus, award the weapons to Odysseus, thereby exciting the bitter resentment of Ajax, who feels himself entitled to this mark of honor both by reason of his renown as a warrior and because he was Achilles' cousin. He resolves to revenge himself on Agamemnon and Menelaus. But Athena intervenes to prevent him from shedding human blood. She afflicts him with madness, driving him to attack a herd of cattle, which he slaughters in the belief that he is destroying his enemies.

It is at this point in the myth that Sophocles' tragedy begins. In the prologue (1–133) the goddess Athena announces that the hero has transgressed the limits set for mortals by the gods. To the horror of Odysseus, whom the Greeks have sent to spy on the hero, the inexorable goddess calls Ajax from his tent and makes him gloat over his grisly deed, in order that Odysseus may see with his own eyes the awful example of Ajax's hubris. Ajax's behavior seems all the more reckless by contrast with Odysseus's sound reasoning (124–26): "I am considering my own affairs no less than his. For I see that all of us who live are but phantoms or insubstantial shadows."

Unlike the Euripidean Heracles (see pp. 99ff.), Ajax, after regaining his sanity and realizing what he has done, sees no alternative to death. His obligation to the men in his contingent (the Salaminian sailors who form the chorus), and his love for his parents and his son, Eurysaces, pale before the inflexible aristocratic standards that govern his existence. He knows of no other way to avoid ignominy but suicide. He is deaf to the soothing words and impassioned pleas of his concubine Tecmessa, who argues that the responsibility that human beings bear for one another outweighs the strictures of his aristocratic code (485ff.). Longing to die, Ajax calls on the eternal night of the underworld (394–409) and the forces of nature around him (412–27):

> Alas, resounding straits, caves by the sea, glade by the shore: long, long indeed have you held me back around Troy. But you will no longer, not while I still breathe: let every sane person know it. O neighboring streams of the Scamander, kindly to the Argives, you will look upon this man no more, a man (I will make this boast) such as Troy never saw among the host of those who came from the land of the Greeks. But now I lie here, thus dishonored.

When Ajax realizes that no one understands why he would rather die than suffer such dishonor, he decides to deceive Tecmessa and the chorus. In a long speech (the so-called "deception speech," 646–92) he tells them that he has come to his senses. Renouncing his obstinacy, he says that, to regain Athena's favor, he will atone for his bloody deed in remote surroundings. But in the event, as everyone in the ancient audience who was familiar with the myth would have anticipated, the atonement of which Ajax ambiguously speaks will be made with his own blood.

The chorus's joyful song (693–718) shows that it has indeed been deceived by Ajax's speech. But its joy is brief. A messenger sent by Teucer, the hero's half-brother, now arrives to tell the chorus and Tecmessa, who at length reappears, of an oracle disclosed by the seer Calchas. If his life is to be saved, says the oracle, Ajax must be detained in his tent today, for only today will he be persecuted by the wrathful goddess. But this revelation comes too late. Ajax has already left his tent; his destiny has been willed by divinity and is irreversible. Tecmessa's reaction is characteristically human. She tells the chorus to find Ajax at once (803ff.). Although Ajax's suicide is all but accomplished, she nevertheless hopes to reach him in time.

By having the chorus leave the stage in the middle of the play (an extremely rare phenomenon in Greek tragedy) Sophocles made it possible for the hero to give his final speech in utter isolation (815–65). He greets Death and then bids farewell to the light; to Salamis, his distant home; and to the Trojan landscape in which he accomplished his heroic exploits: his final words are addressed to inanimate nature (854–65):

> O Death, Death, come now and look at me, though we will meet in Hades and I will speak to you there. I invoke you, light of bright day that now shines, and you, Helius, the charioteer, for the last time. I will never call on you again. O radiance, O sacred plain of Salamis, my native land, O ancestral seat of my hearth, renowned Athens and Athenians reared with me. I invoke you springs and rivers here, and the plains of Troy. Farewell, you who reared me. These words are the last that Ajax cries to you; the rest I will tell to those below in Hades.

The reentry of the chorus (866) marks the beginning of the second half of the play. Even after his death, Ajax continues to influence the actions—indeed, the destiny—of his family and dependents. The Salaminian sailors fear that they may never return home safely without the protection of their leader; Tecmessa fears for her life. Teucer now appears, the bastard despised by all, who has found in Ajax's high reputation a shelter from his enemies. He too dreads what he will have to suffer as a result of his half-brother's suicide (992ff.). The intimates of Ajax are all immediately affected by his death; now they must face the

arrogance and unrelenting hatred of the army chiefs Agamemnon and Menelaus, who seek to prevent the burial of
their dead enemy. The stalemate of opposing wills is
broken by Odysseus (1318ff.). He is portrayed here, as in
the prologue, as a man of reason. When Agamemnon insists that, by attempting to destroy his fellow Greeks, Ajax
forfeited his right to proper burial, Odysseus counters that
this right is guaranteed by divine law and therefore inalien-
able. Antigone employs the same argument; unlike her,
however, Odysseus carries his point.

In *Trachinian Women* the twofold structure of *Ajax* is
inverted. In effect, the one is a mirror image of the other.
Whereas *Ajax* is dominated by the hero's presence in the
first half and by his death and the quarrel over his burial in
the second, in *Trachinian Women* the mere report of the
hero's arrival—keenly anticipated by all in the first two-
thirds of the play (1–970) until he himself appears in the
final third (971–1278)—is paramount. Like Ajax, Heracles
is the central figure despite his being absent from the
stage for much of the play. This structure allowed the poet
to highlight normal human behavior. The audience learns,
first of all, of the distress of a woman who is directly
affected by the heroism of Heracles, her husband, who has
been gone for some fifteen months.

The restlessness and anxiety that overshadow the prologue (1–93) and parodos (94–140) are dispelled when a
messenger enters to announce that Heracles will soon be
coming home (180ff.). The long sequence of scenes that
follows (225–496) is an artful combination of truth and
deception, reality and appearance: Deianeira's jubilation
at the return of her husband is genuine, as is her compassion for Iole, whom she discovers among the women taken
captive by Heracles when he sacked Oechalia (Iole was the
daughter of Eurytus, king of that city). The account given
by Heracles' loyal servant Lichas of his master's campaign
of revenge against King Eurytus is also convincing at first
(248ff.). But when, shortly thereafter (335), a messenger

informs Deianeira that it was love for Iole that moved Heracles to attack Oechalia, the plot takes a new turn. Lichas's account is subsequently proven false, and in the end he comes out with the truth (391ff.). Deianeira plays the understanding wife. Paradoxically, had she maintained the pretense, she might have averted disaster (one is reminded of Ajax's pretense in his deception speech). In fact, she is deeply troubled by the news of her husband's new love. Later (531ff.) she discloses her true feelings to the maidens who make up the chorus: she wants to avoid an open conflict and win back her husband's love by a secret remedy: the centaur Nessus, she explains, once tried to rape her and was struck down by Heracles' arrows; just before he died, he gave her a love charm, telling her that, should she ever have reason to doubt Heracles' love for her, she must smear her husband's clothing with his blood in order to win back his affection.

Too late Deianeira sees through the ruse of the dying Nessus, too late she realizes that the centaur's blood has pernicious powers (663ff.). For she has already had the deadly garment delivered to Heracles. Her dark foreboding is confirmed by the report of her son Hyllus, who tells how Heracles, having donned the garment at a sacrifice, was eaten alive by the poison (734ff.). Speechless, like Eurydice in *Antigone* (1243), Deianeira withdraws into the palace (812). Shortly thereafter Deianeira's nurse enters to tell the chorus of her suicide (871ff.). Before stabbing herself, says the nurse, Deianeira touched household objects and, in utter desperation, leaped onto her marriage bed. These details signify that by reason of her deadly deed Deianeira has forfeited her domain within the house and can no longer see any reason to go on living.

Heracles, by contrast, carried onto the stage in the final scene (971ff.), dies ranting and raving. Even on his deathbed he imposes his will on others. He asks them to deliver him from his agony by burning him alive on Mount Oeta and directs Hyllus to take Iole as his bride. His fury does not cease until Hyllus tells him about the deadly charm, the blood of the centaur. Only then does he see how the two oracles given to him long ago are related, one of which foretold that there would be an end to all his trials, the other that he would die at the hands of one already dead. Having grasped the meaning of the oracles, he bows to his fate (1157ff.).

Antigone

The action of *Antigone* begins one day after the events that form the subject of Aeschylus's *Seven against Thebes.* Eteocles and Polyneices, the sons of King Oedipus, are dead. Creon, as brother of Queen Jocasta and heir apparent, has acceded to the throne. The first act of the new sovereign is to issue a proclamation forbidding the burial of Polyneices on the ground that he is a traitor to his homeland. As in *Ajax,* the primitive custom of leaving the corpse of one's enemy unburied, to be eaten by birds and dogs, is set against the determination of the relatives to do their sacred duty by ensuring that the body of the dead man receives proper burial rites.

Many critics, influenced by the interpretation put forth by Hegel in his *Aesthetics* (p. 3, sec. 3, ch. 3, III c), have seen in *Antigone* a collision of two equally justifiable positions. While Creon claims to be protecting the city, Antigone insists that it is her sacred duty to bury her dead brother. In other words, a conflict has arisen between the interests of the polis and those of the family. In a conversation with Eckermann (March 28, 1827), Goethe took issue with the Hegelian reading, which was widely advocated at the beginning of the nineteenth century:

Besides, Creon acts not from political virtue but from hatred for the dead man. Polyneices' attempt to regain his paternal inheritance, from which he had been forcibly exiled, did not constitute a crime so heinous that his death was not enough and further punishment of his guiltless corpse was required.

A mode of conduct that runs counter to virtue in general should never be called political virtue in the first place. When Creon forbids the burial of Polyneices and not only allows the rotting corpse to contaminate the air but also does not stop dogs and birds of prey from dragging around torn pieces of the dead man and in this way defiling the altars, such conduct, which slights both gods and mortals, is not a political virtue but rather a political crime. Creon antagonizes everyone in the play. He antagonizes the Theban elders who form the chorus. He antagonizes the people in general. He antagonizes Teiresias. He antagonizes his own family. Instead of listening, he persists in his impiety until he has destroyed his entire family and in the end is himself nothing but a shadow.

Goethe's reading was certainly closer to the perspective from which fifth-century Athenian spectators saw the play than was Hegel's. Creon's decree forbidding the burial of Polyneices was inconsistent with the religious feeling of the day. In Athens anyone who failed to bury a dead relative was liable to the curse of the Buzygae (a prominent priestly family). By issuing a decree meant to keep Antigone and Ismene from carrying out their duty, Creon shows himself to be a despot even before his entrance. This initial impression is borne out by what he says and does in the course of the play. Unlike Pelasgus in Aeschylus's *Suppliants*, Creon does not seek the opinion of the people. Instead, he consults with the aristocratic council of Theban elders who form the chorus of the play. He scents treason, subversion, and bribery in every quarter. He shows a lack of trust that is antithetical to the conduct of people in a democracy, at least as that conduct is idealized in the oration that Thucydides puts in the mouth of Pericles

(2.37). "Advantage" (*kerdos*) is a recurrent theme in Creon's speeches. To his mind gain is the one and only aim of human action. When Antigone tries to explain to him why she felt compelled to bury her brother, he turns a deaf ear (450ff.). Absorbed in his role as ruler of Thebes, he indulges in aphorisms and banalities (473ff.). He is deaf to the entreaties of his son Haemon (683ff.), who tries to dissuade his father from making a rash decision. He accuses his son of uxoriousness (740, 756) and stresses that in Thebes he is the absolute ruler (738): "Do people not hold the city to belong to the ruler?" He is even deaf to the revelations of the seer Teiresias, who, warned by unfavorable omens, urges him to desist from his fatal course and allow the dead man to be buried (998ff.). In his folly he supposes even Teiresias to be a venal traitor (1033ff.). Creon is so severely afflicted by *atē* (bewilderment)—which causes him to see bribery, treason, and treachery everywhere he looks—that he neglects to venerate the gods and their spokesman Teiresias. It is only after the seer has cursed him for his obstinacy, predicting that one of his own will die in consequence of his impious conduct, that Creon finally comes to his senses. But it is too late (cf. 1270): a messenger announces that Antigone and Haemon have already taken their own lives (1183ff.). Quietly, like Deianeira in *Trachinian Women*, Creon's wife Eurydice goes off (1243) to hang herself (1278–80). Like an Aeschylean hero, the broken ruler finds himself at the mercy of an uncompromising destiny that has bewildered his mind and brought him to ruin (1271–76): "Ah me, in misery I have learned! Then, then did a god with his great weight strike me on my head and shake me on my wild course, ah me, overturning and trampling on my happiness. Alas, alas, the toils of mortals, unhappy toils!"

Creon comes to realize, after great suffering, that he has acted wrongly. Whereas his character undergoes change, that of Antigone is static from the outset. She has made the irrevocable decision to carry out the burial of her

brother, alone if necessary, and even if no one else sees
that her plan is right and necessary. Her claim to absolute
right and the autonomy of her character (cf. 821) emerge
clearly from her conversation with her sister Ismene,
which forms the prologue of the play (1–99). Antigone
appeals to her sense of duty as sister of Polyneices, while
Ismene hides behind Creon's prohibition. Ismene stresses
that it is unlike a woman to do battle with a man (61f.) and
does not want to provoke further the destiny that has
already struck the house of Oedipus so cruelly, whereas
Antigone puts the values that she espouses in absolute
terms and is unwilling to compromise.

The opening dialogue between the two sisters is fraught
with tension. It begins as an amicable exchange but soon
erupts into a fierce quarrel leading ultimately to Antigone's isolation.

Antigone acts in the conviction that what she is doing
is right and therefore does not equivocate when she is
caught trying to bury her brother for the second time. She
listens quietly to the guard's boastful report, then con-
fesses to her deed without hesitation (435), emphasizing
that she deliberately contravened Creon's decree, because,
she says, the unwritten laws that govern her actions are to
be valued more highly than any king's decrees. Having
resolved to take the course that she believes to be right,
and to do so alone, she now rejects Ismene's help, who
incriminates herself out of love for her sister. "Unwept,
friendless, and unwedded" (876), Antigone is led away to
die in the knowledge that she has done the right thing
(891ff.).

The remaining characters — Ismene, Haemon, the guard,
and the chorus — are situated between the poles embodied
by Creon and Antigone, and it is on them that their atti-
tudes and actions depend. Ismene is torn between fear of
Creon and love of her sister. In the prologue her fear of the
ruler proves stronger and makes her act in conformity
with his will. But when she sees Antigone's predicament,

she can no longer resist the impulse to help her sister and stands solidly behind her without considering the danger that loomed so large in her argument against Antigone's plan in the prologue. Unlike her sister, Ismene does not tend toward the fundamental and irrevocable; instead, she attempts to reconcile Creon and Antigone, to break down the rigid barriers that divide them by appealing to their familial feelings with an allusion to Haemon's betrothal to Antigone (568ff.). She represents the ordinary person, a foil to her sister's extraordinary character.

At first, Haemon merely embodies the tension between his love for his father and his love for his betrothed. Only when he realizes that Creon will not listen to reason (726ff.) does he openly side with Antigone.

The guard represents another "ordinary person," who, unlike Ismene, does not belong to the ruling family. He shows how such a person behaves under autocratic rule. Cringing in fear before Creon, he hesitates to report that an unknown person has tried to bury Polyneices, prevaricating (223ff.) until he has obtained assurance from Creon that he will not be punished (244). Later, when he has success to report, he no sooner appears than he blurts out the news of Antigone's capture (384) and parades the service that he has rendered in apprehending her. The two guard scenes expose an oppression that is symptomatic of autocracy. The Athenian spectators of the fifth century saw *Antigone* against the background of their political experience and thus were aware that while such behavior as the guard's is possible in a political system in which the lives of the citizens depend on the arbitrary will of one man, it is not in a democracy such as Athens enjoyed, in which all the citizens work, at least theoretically, towards the common good and are free to voice their opinions without fear. Indirectly, then, insofar as it shows that dark side of autocracy, the play is extolling the Athenian democracy.

The attitude of the chorus is not unlike that of the guard. As Creon's advisory council its members occupy a

higher social station than the guard and therefore are not
directly affected by Creon's decree. Nevertheless the Theban elders avoid taking a firm position and only now and
then indicate on whose side they stand. Thus, in their initial state of surprise when they first learn from the guard
that Polyneices has been buried, they describe the deed as
"caused by god," an expression that carries with it the
implication that Creon's decree is "godless." Apart from
this passing remark, they remain evasive in their choral
songs. The songs abound in general reflections that often
exhibit connections with the dramatic events, even if
these connections are, in keeping with their attitude,
ambivalent—as, for example, in the final strophe of the
first stasimon (368–75): "He who upholds the laws of the
land and the justice of the gods to which he is bound by
oath is exalted in his city, but he is without a city who
dares to keep company with injustice. May whoever does
these things neither join me at my hearth nor think as I
do." At one level the adjective *apolis* 'without a city' (370)
applies to Antigone, who defies the authority of civil law;
at another level it also applies to Creon, who, by issuing
his decree, has shown contempt for divine law, the "justice
of the gods to which he is bound by oath" (369). Only when
the Theban elders realize that Creon, having given
thought to Teiresias's curse, is beginning to doubt the pro-
priety of his ban do they at last take a stand and call on
him to yield (1100ff.).

With *Antigone* Sophocles has reached the phase in his
career in which he abandons the strict diptych form. The
point at which Antigone exits to her death (943) marks a
break, it is true, but since Creon remains onstage throughout the entire play, one can no longer speak of discontinu-
ity, at least as far as his character is concerned. The
complex action and the various connections between the
dramatis personae, which led Hegel to describe *Antigone*
as a "most splendid and satisfying work of art," set this
play apart from the two earlier pieces, *Ajax* and *Trachinian*

Women, which are more monologic and are structured
rigidly and without transition.

The Oedipus Plays:
Oedipus the King — Oedipus at Colonus

A few years after the production of *Antigone* Sophocles
wrote his masterpiece, *Oedipus the King.* The subject is
again taken from the Theban cycle. A terrible plague has
descended on Thebes. In their despair the citizens turn to
King Oedipus (1–83), who once saved the city from disaster by solving the riddle of the Sphinx and in return was
awarded the throne as well as the hand of the widowed
queen Jocasta. The oracle of the god Apollo, obtained at
Oedipus's behest by his brother-in-law Creon, promises
salvation for the city. But there is a condition. Only if the
murderer of Laius is found and punished can the blood
guilt now hanging heavily over Thebes be purged (95ff.).
Oedipus at once initiates a search. Laius, he learns from
Creon, was struck down by brigands on his way to Delphi,
as the sole surviving eyewitness reported (122f.). Oedipus
comes closer to the truth when in his reply to Creon he
speaks of only one brigand, but goes astray in assuming
that this man was an assassin hired by Theban conspira-
tors. He becomes preoccupied with this assumption and
presses the seer Teiresias for information. Teiresias, who
knows the awful truth, evades his questions, and the king
suspects him of collusion with the murderer. When Oedipus goes so far as to denounce Teiresias as the killer of
Laius, the seer can contain his rage no longer and retorts,
"You are yourself the murderer whom you seek!" (353,
362). As Oedipus becomes more and more entangled
in his misconceptions, accusing even Creon of complicity with the seer, Teiresias reveals the whole truth to
him. In his wrath Oedipus is deaf to the prophet's words
(447–62):

I have said what I came to say and will be going, not
fearing your countenance. For you cannot hurt me. I
will tell you: this man whom you have long been seeking, making threats and proclaiming an inquest into
the murder of Laius, this man is here, and though said
to be a stranger from another city, he will be shown to
be a native Theban and will not be pleased with his
fortune. For, changed from one who has seen to one
who is blind, from a rich man to a beggar, he will journey to a strange land, feeling the ground before him
with a staff. And he will prove to be at once brother
and father to the children with whom he lives, at
once son and husband of the woman of whom he was
born, sowing what his father sowed, murdering his
father. Go inside and think about these things, and if
you find that I have not spoken the truth, consider me
to have no mind for prophecy.

Just as the notion (and at first it is no more than a notion)
that Laius was killed by a hired assassin hardens into fact
in Oedipus's mind during his clash with Teiresias, so his
suspicion of Creon's complicity hardens into certainty in
the next episode (513ff.). Jocasta intervenes between the
quarreling men and defends her brother against the allegations of her enraged husband. Oedipus tells her that a seer
has charged him with the murder of Laius. She tries to
impugn the charge by questioning the reliability of prophecies (711–24):

An oracle once came to Laius, I will not say from
Phoebus himself, but from his ministers, according to
which it was fated that he die at the hands of a child
who would be born of him and me. Laius, you will
remember, was killed by foreign brigands at a place
where three roads met—this, at least, is what people
say. Anyway, not three days had passed since the
child's birth, when Laius yoked its feet together and
had it thrown, by the hands of others, on an untrodden

mountain. And thereafter Apollo did not bring it about
that the child become the murderer of his father or
that Laius suffer the terrible thing that he feared at
the hands of his child. This is the shape that the oracles gave to things. So pay heed to none of them!

Instead of putting her husband's mind at ease, Jocasta does
just the opposite. Her passing reference to the fork in the
road (716) causes Oedipus profound concern. Just as the
mention of Nessus's name enables Heracles to understand
his destiny in *Trachinian Women* (1141), so the passing reference to the fork in the road rends asunder, with one
stroke, the curtain of semblance for Oedipus. Like a pros-
ecutor interrogating a witness, he questions Jocasta about
the location of the fork, the time of the murder, and the
appearance of Laius. When he hears that the king was
accompanied by five men, he cries out: "Alas! Now it is
clear!" (754). To his confused wife Oedipus explains what
has upset him and why he is asking her so many questions
(771ff.): someone once taunted him at a banquet, saying
that he was not the true son of Polybus and Merope, the
king and queen of Corinth. To find out for certain, he set
out for Delphi, where Apollo made it known to him that
he would murder his father and beget children by his
mother. To thwart the oracle, he resolved to avoid Corinth
from that moment forward. He came to a place not far
from Delphi where one road branched into two. There a
man drove him off the road with his horse and carriage.
Enfuriated, Oedipus killed him and all his retainers but
one, who fled for his life. As the sole surviving eyewitness
this man is Oedipus's last glimmer of hope. If the eyewitness confirms that Laius was killed by a band of robbers,
Oedipus can pronounce himself free from guilt. In an
attempt to reassure Oedipus, Jocasta again casts doubt on
the reliability of oracles. For, according to the old prophecy, Laius was supposed to have perished at the hands of
his son, and he died long ago.

The truth is about to come crashing down on Oedipus and Jocasta, and their reactions are masterfully drawn. In view of what he has learned from Jocasta, Oedipus must take himself for Laius's murderer. Still, he clings to the false report that the king was slain not by one man but by a band of robbers, and sends for the sole eyewitness of the killing in the hope that this man may exonerate him (836–37). His first reaction to Jocasta's reference to the fork in the road is telling. In his initial alarm, he realizes that what Teiresias told him is true: he himself is the man whom he has been seeking (747). But he does not say a word about the seer's other allegations—that he has murdered his father and married his mother, though he has just finished relating to Jocasta the predictions of the oracle of Apollo, which foretold the same doom.

After the climatic final scene of the second episode the process of discovery is retarded by the unexpected arrival of an aged messenger from Corinth (924ff.), who reports that Polybus has died. This piece of news seems to prove that the first part of the oracle has not been fulfilled, as Oedipus's father died of natural causes. But what of the second part? When Oedipus shows concern over the second prediction of the oracle, the Corinthian, in an attempt to put his mind at rest, informs him that he is not the biological child of Polybus and Merope but a foundling raised by them as their own son. The old man explains that a babe was once given to him by a Theban herdsman of Mount Cithaeron, and that he brought the infant to the king and queen of Corinth, who, being themselves childless, were glad to adopt the boy. This Theban herdsman, the chorus leader suspects (1051–53), must be none other than the eyewitness of Laius's murder for whom Oedipus has sent. Jocasta, who in the meantime has realized the whole truth, tries to prevent him from making further inquiries (1056ff.). But Oedipus's desire to learn the truth about his engendering lies too deep within him.

The truth is revealed to Oedipus in a brief episode

(1110–85). An old man is led onstage, and the Corinthian confirms that this man is indeed the Theban shepherd who once gave him a child on Mount Cithaeron. Oedipus interrogates the old man. Like Lichas in *Trachinian Women*, who is as intent on hiding the truth as the messenger is on effecting its disclosure (400ff.), the old Theban makes Oedipus wring the truth from him under threat of torture. His words thrust Oedipus into an abyss of dreadful recognition (1182–85): "Oh! Oh! It is fulfilled, all of it, clear to be seen! O light, may I now look on you for the last time, since I have been shown to be sprung from parents who never should have been mine, to have lain with a woman with whom I never should have lain, to have killed one whom I never should have killed!"

Up to its peripety (1110–85) the play has dramatized the process of discovering the truth; henceforth, in the exodos (1223–1530), it will dramatize the consequences of that discovery. A servant emerges from the palace to relate that Jocasta has hanged herself and Oedipus has gouged out his eyes. Then the blinded Oedipus himself appears. What follows is an *ecce homo* scene in which the events of the play are reviewed from a theological perspective. Whereas Ajax (in *Ajax*), Heracles (in *Trachinian Women*), and Creon (in *Antigone*) deserve, in the Aeschylean sense, the adversity that they suffer because they have committed acts of hubris, disregarding divine law and the limits that the gods have imposed on human conduct, it is difficult to see why Oedipus must suffer the worst adversity imaginable when he has done nothing to deserve it. Apollo was the author of his suffering (1329–30); why the god has made him suffer, however, is not known. The gods are too distant, too great, and too powerful to be understood by mortals, who therefore can see no meaning in their suffering. The divine lies beyond the horizon of human understanding, although the divine will and a kind of knowledge of the divine have been made known to mortals through oracular utterances and the revelations of seers. In their minds mortals see alternatives where there are none, options that are ruled out by the wording of the oracles; they impose conditions on the unconditional and cling to hope as a last resort. "Hope" (*elpis*), so fatal to human understanding, is a key word in the play. Used from the beginning (121) in the context of Oedipus's search for Laius's murderer, its significance becomes even more evident when the chorus, in its entrance song, elevates the idea to the status of a divinity (158) on a par with the Olympian gods. It was hope that led Laius to have his newborn son exposed in the mountains to thwart Apollo's oracle and avoid being killed by his own son; it was hope that led Oedipus to believe that by never again setting foot in Corinth he could avert the fate that had been prophesied to him by the Delphic god. The third oracle, the one received by Creon on Oedipus's behalf, in effect catalyzes the dramatic action, bringing about what Schiller, in a letter to Goethe (dated October 2, 1797), called the "tragic analysis": the fateful search for Laius's murderer and so also for Oedipus's true engendering. And just as these two investigations, these two courses of action ultimately become one, so the three oracles contain a single terrible truth: the farther Oedipus progresses in his search for Laius's murderer at the prompting of the third oracle, the closer he comes to the truth of the first two oracles and the deeper he penetrates into the past. And the closer he comes to what he imagines to be truth and salvation, the closer he comes to the abyss of self-knowledge.

The plot of *Oedipus the King* seems, more than any other work, imbued with tragic suffering. Wherever in the hero's destiny one's gaze is fixed, it is met by that unity of salvation and destruction which is a characteristic feature of all that is tragic. For it is not his destruction that is tragic but the fact that his salvation changes to destruction; the tragic lies not in the ruin of the hero but in the fact that man goes to ruin down the path that he took to escape it. The essential heroic experience, which is confirmed with every step he takes, gives way only at the last moment to another: the realization that it is at the end of this path that salvation and redemption are found. (P. Szondi, "Versuch über das Tragische," in *Schriften I* [Frankfurt, 1978] 213.)

Yet it is not in *Oedipus the King* that Sophocles' hero arrives at "salvation and redemption" but *Oedipus at Colonus*, written shortly before his death some thirty years later. The play's intricate plot, numerous repetitions, and excessive length show that it is a late work.

In *Oedipus at Colonus* the divine is present from the beginning: Oedipus has received an oracle from Apollo, according to which he will find his final resting place in the sacred precinct of the Eumenides in the Athenian deme of Colonus (84ff.). Before he can attain his prophesied end, however, two conditions must be met. First the Athenians, represented by their king Theseus, must grant Oedipus asylum. Then an immediate threat from Thebes must be averted: Creon wants to bring Oedipus, who is attended by Antigone, back to Thebes, allegedly because he regards Oedipus's degrading circumstances as a disgrace to Thebes and the Theban ruling house (728ff.). The true reason, however, as Oedipus has learned earlier from Ismene (324ff.), is that, in the dispute over the Theban throne between Eteocles and Polyneices, an oracle foretells victory to whoever has Oedipus in his possession. To give teeth to his threats, Creon has Antigone and Ismene abducted (818ff.), but Theseus succeeds in restoring both daughters to Oedipus unharmed (1119ff.). In a scene parallel to the clash between Oedipus and Creon, Polyneices attempts to win his father over to his side (1249ff.). But Oedipus is adamant towards his son, as he was towards

Creon earlier, because he realizes that it is only thirst for power and not kindness that brings Polyneices to him.

Only after these external dangers have been averted can the oracle be fulfilled (1456ff.). Now, when his end has been announced by peals of thunder, the old blind man is no longer in need of help from others; he confidently goes ahead of Theseus to the place where he is to find the death for which he has longed (1588ff.). When Oedipus had performed the ritual ablutions, a messenger reports to the chorus, the voice of a god rang out (1628f.): "O Oedipus, Oedipus, why do we hesitate to go forth? Long indeed have you been made to tarry." Thus, the end of *Oedipus at Colonus* offers a solution to the problems that *Oedipus the King* left unresolved. If the earlier Oedipus play ended with the self-blinding of a guilty and yet guiltless man and the realization that the gods remain unfathomable for mortals, *Oedipus at Colonus* resolves the opposition between god and mortal in the fraternal "we" with which Oedipus is summoned by the god. There exists a kind divinity who has mercy on those who have suffered much and grants them death not as an inevitable, harsh destiny but as a blessing:

> Having shown us the blinding and the fall of Oedipus, the terrible downfall and the mutual fratricide of his sons, the long suffering of the old man and his loyal nurse and daughter, Sophocles is able to show us his death as a journey to the placable gods in a light so bright that he leaves us with a sense of a gentle emotion, more melancholy than painful, and nothing more. Resolutions of this type are common enough among ancients and moderns, but only rarely are they so great and beautiful. (Friedrich von Schlegel, "Zur Geschichte der alten und neuen Literatur," in *Kritische Schriften*, 3rd ed. [Munich, 1970] 610.)

79

Electra

In its structure and plot Sophocles' *Electra* is essentially different from Aeschylus's *Choephori* and Euripides' *Electra* (for the dates see p. 59), the two other versions of the story that have come down to us. Whereas in the Aeschylean and Euripidean versions Orestes recognizes his sister at the outset (*Choephori* 16f.; *Electra* 112ff.) and declares himself to Electra in the first episode, Sophocles defers the recognition, or *anagnōrismos*, to the final third of his play (1174ff.). Orestes suspects that the woman whose plaintive cries he hears emanating from the palace could be Electra (80ff.), but when the old tutor who attends him and Pylades urges that they first make a sacrificial offering at Agamemnon's grave (82–85), there is no "eavesdropping scene" (see p. 46) in preparation for the anagnōrismos, as in the other two plays.

Because of this structural change, the Sophoclean Electra herself falls victim to the intrigue launched by Orestes and the old man. When the old man reports to Clytemnestra the news of Orestes' death (680ff.), Electra collapses amid the gibes of her mother. This false report, meant to put Clytemnestra and Aegisthus off their guard, has a devastating effect on Electra, for it dashes the hope, lately nourished by her mother's ominous dream (417ff.), that had made life with Clytemnestra and Aegisthus in the palace at Mycenae—where she had been their living bad conscience, so to speak—only just bearable.

At this extremely desperate moment Chrysothemis brings her sister a lock of hair which, she supposes, proves that Orestes has returned to Argos (871ff.). To her mind the lock, which she discovered on Agamemnon's bedecked tomb, can only be Orestes'. Electra, however, convinced that her brother is dead, dismisses it as an offering left by some friend of her dead brother. The Sophoclean Electra thus rejects a clue which her Aeschylean counterpart had not called into question (*Choephori* 167ff.).

There is no mention of the other recognition tokens of Aeschylus's play, the footprint and the embroidered garment. The protagonist of Euripides' *Electra* also denies the validity of these tokens as corroborative evidence in a rationalistic argument that is probably meant to be a parody of Aeschylus's recognition scene (*Electra* 508ff.).

After the news of her brother's death Electra is left with nothing but intense hate. It is hate that sustains her now, hate that even drives her to plot revenge on her father's murderers. In a splendid display of eloquence, Electra, like Antigone in her attempt to win over Ismene, tries to persuade her sister Chrysothemis to be her ally in the murder. Knowing that all her sister wants is an ordinary life as a married woman, she reminds her (964–66): "Aegisthus is not so ill-advised a man as ever to allow your offspring, or mine, a manifest bane to him, to flourish." As in her first clash with Chrysothemis (328ff.), Electra is unable to overcome her sister's resistance. Chrysothemis, for her part, cannot comprehend her sister's intransigence. Like Ismene, she prefers a quiet life to one of action. She has come to terms with the powers that be (339f.): to her, outer freedom is more important than inner independence.

Thus, Electra, like Antigone, is compelled to undertake the deed on her own (1019f.). She becomes the protagonist of the play, while in Aeschylus's *Choephori* the central role is assumed by Orestes, and in Euripides' *Electra* and *Orestes* by both brother and sister. Only the anagnōrismos in the next scene makes Electra change her plan and unite her purpose with that of her brother.

The particular appeal of Sophocles' *Electra* for the fifth-century audience would have consisted in the fact that, because the recognition of brother and sister is postponed, Electra herself falls victim to the stratagem and in desperation resolves to kill her mother and Aegisthus on her own. For a moment one wonders whether the oracle of Apollo, to which Orestes refers in the prologue, will be fulfilled or not. For, according to the oracle, Orestes is "alone and without a host of men at arms to carry out by stealth and artifice the just slaughter" (36f.).

There is another essential difference between Sophocles' play and the other two versions: the valuation of the matricide. Orestes never wavers in the prosecution of his plan to avenge his father. He believes, on the strength of Apollo's oracle, that he has been sent on a mission by the gods to be the "purifier of the house" who, by murdering Clytemnestra and Aegisthus, will expiate the blood guilt that has stained the Tantalids and the palace in which their atrocities have taken place. He never hesitates. He needs neither to be reminded of his divine mandate by his friend Pylades, as the Aeschylean Orestes does, nor to be urged on by his sister, as does the Orestes of Euripides' play.

After the matricide we hear nothing of the pangs of conscience that, in the form of Erinyes, torment Orestes in *Choephori*, nothing of the reproaches that brother and sister, overcome with revulsion at the sight of their mother's corpse, hurl at Apollo in Euripides. It is just this familiarity with the myth and with its treatment by Aeschylus and Euripides that would have made Sophocles' *Electra* an open-ended play for the fifth-century audience, and that would have caused that audience to consider whether "Apollo prophesied well" (1425) or not, and to ponder how Orestes and Electra will be able to go on living in the knowledge of their terrible deed.

Philoctetes

Philoctetes was produced in 409. The play is in many respects similar to *Electra*, which had been staged only a few years earlier. Its protagonist is a lonely figure. Banished from society, he is compelled to fend for himself in a situation that ill befits his aristocratic origins. His suffering arises not from the will of some divinity or from his own arrogance, but from the collision of opposing human interests.

The story is taken from the Theban Cycle. While the Greeks, on their way to Troy, are sojourning on the island of Chryse, Philoctetes is bitten in the foot by a snake. The stench from his festering sore vexes the Greek army so much that its commanders decide, at the suggestion of Odysseus, to abandon the ailing man on the island of Lemnos. There he ekes out a wretched existence in utter solitude. Just as Electra is sustained by hatred for her mother and Aegisthus, so Philoctetes is sustained by hatred for the Atreidae and Odysseus. His loathing feeds on the agonies that fill his days on that desolate island.

Once, after ten years of loneliness and embitterment, he trusts a young man, Achilles' young son Neoptolemus — who, like Philoctetes, belongs to the aristocracy and appears, at least, to share his aristocratic ideals and even his hatred for the Atreidae and Odysseus (343ff.) — and is deceived. Even more bitter now than he was before, Philoctetes breaks off all communication with others; he is deaf to the soothing words of the chorus, deaf to Neoptolemus's arguments. An oracle foretells that he will be cured if he goes to Troy. But he would sooner do without the cure than be in the service of the Greeks.

Opposite Philoctetes the inexorable is Odysseus, a power politician for whom only the facts count and who does not shrink from employing deceit if he thinks that there is an advantage to be gained by it, for whom there are no absolute norms and values, and for whom oracles are a welcome means of justifying morally dubious conduct and of supporting morally dubious arguments. He is not unlike the clever men whose behavior is described by Thucydides in his analysis of political morality during the Peloponnesian War (3.82).

Neoptolemus is located between these two poles. He is induced by Odysseus to worm his way into Philoctetes' confidence by devious means and to this end must deny his own honest character for one day (54ff.). Philoctetes believes Neoptolemus's false tale, in part because he sees his own fate reflected in Neoptolemus's mistreatment at the hands of the commanders of the Greek army. Overwhelmed, finally, with pity for the sick man, Neoptolemus promises Philoctetes on his word of honor that he will bring him back home to Greece. In so doing, however, he disregards both the interests of the Greeks, who have set their hopes on him, and his promise to Odysseus. He said that he would bring Philoctetes to Troy; now, no matter what he decides, he must break his word. Yet it is wrong to say that Neoptolemus is the central figure in the play simply because he must make this tragic decision; rather, the central figure is Philoctetes, an unchanging character of extraordinary proportions. For such a man, just as for Antigone and Electra, there are no alternatives because his character is unchanging; there is only the one way that he believes to be right. Only the weaker figures are encumbered with tragic decisions; only they can act rightly or wrongly; only they have doubts; only they, like Creon in *Antigone*, come to understanding through suffering.

Two motifs define the action of the play: the oracle of the Trojan seer Helenus, which stipulates that Philoctetes must sail to Troy of his own free will if the city is to fall that same summer in accordance with the divine purpose (1331ff.), and the ever imminent frustration of that purpose through the intrigue and obstinacy of mortals. It is shown in the course of the action that Odysseus and Neoptolemus have been well aware of all the terms of the oracle from the beginning. When the sailors who form the chorus advise their master Neoptolemus to take the bow and sail off without the sleeping Philoctetes, the youth answers in dactylic hexameters, in which he quotes, as it were, the oracle (839–42): "True, he cannot hear a thing, but I see that our hunt for this bow will be in vain if we sail off without him. For this garland is his, and the god bade us bring it. It is a foul disgrace to boast mendaciously of things that cannot be." But instead of yielding to the will of the gods, Odysseus tries to prepare the ground for destiny on his own. More than once it seems as if the oracle will not be fulfilled, especially when, at the end of the play, Neoptolemus promises Philoctetes that he will bring him home (1402ff.). At this point Heracles—it was from Heracles that Philoctetes once received his bow, in return for lighting the dying hero's funeral pyre on Mount Oeta—appears ex machina to ensure that the divine purpose prevails over mortal obstinacy (1409ff.).

Implicit in the deus ex machina scene is a deeply pessimistic view of human knowledge. Even when knowledge of the divine is vouchsafed to them through oracles and prophecies, mortals try to force these revelations into the narrow range of their own understanding. In their arrogance they would—if they were all that mattered—thwart the designs of the gods: Neoptolemus would have brought Philoctetes home; Troy would never have been taken. In the fictive context of the play the poet can still bring everything to a satisfactory conclusion by means of the device of the deus ex machina, as Euripides was to do in his *Orestes* one year later. But by making Heracles' epiphany appear as if it were superimposed on the action, Sophocles makes it clear that only in the fictive context is a resolution, a happy ending, possible. In reality, it is human obstinacy and malice that win out.

The Heroic Personality and
the Problem of Human Knowledge

According to Plutarch, Sophocles himself distinguished three phases of growth in his poetic career. In the first he freed his verse from Aeschylean influence; in the second he rid his style of harshness and artificiality; in the third he perfected it by imparting to each of his characters the manner of speech most appropriate to his or her nature.

Whereas the tragedies of Aeschylus expound a theodicy, an argument for an order willed by the gods, those of Sophocles focus on human beings under the strain of acute crisis. Circumstances compel his protagonists to extraordinary action. They are convinced that what they are doing is right—indeed, the only right thing to do. The temperament of an Electra, an Antigone, or an Oedipus contrasts sharply with that of a Chrysothemis, an Ismene, or a Jocasta, who, unwilling to risk the quiet of their unremarkable lives, accommodate themselves to the status quo. If in Aeschylus mortals are still situated within the divine order, in Sophocles they are "severed from the universe of the gods"; their lives are struck by the will of divinity as by lightning; and when it strikes, they face "something wholly unlike themselves, incomprehensible, an emanation from a world other than their own" (Karl Reinhardt, *Sophokles* [Frankfurt, 1933] 13).

In each of the seven tragedies that survive, Sophocles has a god communicate his will to mortals, whether through an oracle or a soothsayer. Entangled in their hopes, his characters are unable to recognize the divine will. Instead they force it into accord with their own imperfect understanding, believing that through thought and action they can avert a destiny that cannot be averted.

IV

EURIPIDES

Life and Works

Ancient biographers tended to evaluate the works of the tragic poets on the basis of details of their lives and, in particular, to take the ridicule of comedy at face value. Consequently, valuable testimonia have been obfuscated by gossip and anecdotes. This tendency is nowhere more evident than in the biographies of Euripides, who received his share of ridicule from his contemporary Aristophanes.

Only a few facts about Euripides' life are known or can be deduced with any degree of probability. He was born between 485 and 480 B.C. on the island of Salamis; he was given his first chorus—that is, the performing rights for his debut at the Great Dionysia—in 455; his first victory came in 441. Like Aeschylus, Euripides also left Athens (in 408) to spend the last years of his life at the court of the Macedonian king Archelaus in Pella. He died in 406, shortly before the Great Dionysia (roughly February/March). At the news of Euripides' death, Sophocles had his chorus appear at the *proagōn* (see p. 10) unadorned with the garlands that were customary on that occasion.

To judge from these scanty data, which are all that remain once the gossip and the anecdotes have been swept aside, Euripides, unlike Aeschylus and Sophocles, never held a political or religious office nor took part as an Athenian soldier in a military operation. He seems to have been detached from public life, and this detachment left its mark on his work. Whereas Sophocles, even during the crisis of the final stage of the Peloponnesian War, never lost faith in either Athens or its democracy and, although he gave a hint of skepticism in *Philoctetes*, left a memorial to his native city in *Oedipus at Colonus* (57f.), Euripides suffused his late works with pessimism.

It was very probably this pessimism that made Euripides leave his home in 408. There may have been another reason: as a tragic poet he had not known the measure of success with the judges, and so too with the public, that Aeschylus and Sophocles had enjoyed before him. Although he took part in the dramatic competition twenty-two times, and thus composed at least eighty-eight plays (to which we may add two plays not performed in Athens: *Archelaus*, which was composed in Pella, and *Andromache*), he took first place only four times. It was only after his death that he came to be regarded as "the tragic poet par excellence" (*ho tragikōtatos*, as Aristotle describes him, *Poetics* 1453a 29). His subjects, methods of composition, and dramatic techniques had an enduring influence on the poets of fourth-century tragedy as well as on those of Middle and New Comedy in the fourth and third centuries. Through the Roman playwrights Plautus, Terence, and Seneca he left his mark on the whole subsequent tradition of European drama.

One ancient view of Euripides' work is reflected in the comedies of his contemporary Aristophanes. In *Frogs*, for example, he is charged with having represented his characters in a manner incongruous with their heroic dignity. The heroes and heroines of myth were portrayed in a crassly realistic manner as ordinary fifth-century men and women. This redefinition of the heroic in terms of the ordinary is best illustrated by *Electra*. In *Telephus* (438),

88

which is not extant, Euripides made the hero Telephus appear on stage dressed in rags. The scene was parodied by Aristophanes in his *Archarnians* and *Women at the Thesmophoria*. Euripides is also ridiculed for having couched banal tales in pathetic diction and lyric form. In a word, he is said to have offended repeatedly against the lofty nature, the "decorum" (*prepon*) of tragedy. Aristophanes had profound insight into the theatrical sensibilities of his day and could see that what Euripides was undertaking, particularly in his later plays, was a tightrope walk. In departing from traditional story patterns, in innovating forms of expression, in exploiting all the linguistic and musical resources at his disposal, so that at times his diction might seem bizarre, his lyrics manneristic, he was only one step away, as the parodies of Aristophanes show, from the ridiculous.

The dated plays provide a framework within which the others can be arranged chronologically. In the case of *Alcestis* (438), *Medea* (431), *Hippolytus* (428), *Trojan Women* (415), *Helen* (412), and *Orestes* (408), the date of production is known from documentary evidence. *Bacchae* and *Iphigeneia at Aulis* were produced after the author's death in 406 B.C. *Rhesus* was written by an unknown author of the fourth century.

Metrical statistics have proven to be a reliable method of establishing a relative chronology for the undated plays. The chief criterion is the frequency of resolutions in passages written in iambic trimeter, the meter used for dialogue in Attic drama. By "resolution" is meant that in the sequence ∪− the long (−) is resolved into two shorts (∪∪). It has been demonstrated that, among the plays that can be securely dated, the late ones show a higher percentage of resolutions in the iambic line than do the earlier ones. Over the years, then, Euripides allowed himself increasing latitude in the composition of the iambic line. In the early plays the proportion is quite low. For example, in *Alcestis* (438) and *Medea* (431) it is 6.7 and 7.3 percent, respectively.

In his later work, however, it increases to 35.5 percent in *Helen* (412) and 49.3 percent in *Orestes* (408). The undated plays can be assigned, on the basis of their percentages, to periods defined by the *termini post quem* and *ante quem* supplied by the securely dated plays. Thus, *Children of Heracles* falls within the years 431–428; *Andromache, Hecuba,* and *Suppliant Women* all belong to the 420s; *Electra* (419?) was produced before *Heracles* (ca. 416) and *Trojan Women* (415); *Ion, Iphigeneia among the Taurians,* and *Phoenician Women* must be later than *Trojan Women* but earlier than *Orestes* (408), and the satyr play *Cyclops* probably belongs to the same period.

Three Women: Alcestis, Medea, and Phaedra

In Aristophanes' *Women at the Thesmophoria* (411) the women of Athens assemble at the Thesmophoria, a festival held in honor of the goddesses Demeter and Persephone, to pronounce judgment against Euripides for writing plays that give women a bad name. The comic condemnation of Euripides as a misogynist and the charge leveled against him by Aristophanes in *Frogs* (1043ff.), that he has corrupted the Athenians by showing illicit and shameful passions in his tragedies, can be traced back to his oft-cited portrayal of Phaedra, whom Euripides examined in the two plays that bear the title *Hippolytus,* of which only the second (428) is extant. In keeping with the tendency of comedy to simplify, Aristophanes singles out Phaedra, without doing justice to the diversity and complexity of Euripides' treatment of women. Indeed, many Euripidean plays of the forties and thirties focus on the fate, the social standing, the feelings, and the passions of a woman. In play after play, the poet illuminated the relations between men and women from various perspectives. The three figures of Alcestis, Medea, and Phaedra represent three different interpretations of this topic.

Alcestis was the fourth play in a tetralogy that included *Cretan Women, Alcmaeon at Psophis,* and *Telephus,* and thus took the place usually occupied by the satyr play. It is probably no accident that *Alcestis,* with its happy ending and the figures of the foiled villain (Death) and the carousing, carefree hero (Heracles), exhibits some of the typical features of satyr drama (see pp. 11f.). The play is divided into two parts. In the first (1–746) Alcestis dies and preparations are made for her burial. The chorus of old men leave the stage to join the funeral procession. Their exit marks a clear break—indeed, a drastic turn in the action—since in Greek drama it is very unusual for the chorus to leave the orchestra during the action (see p. 50 on *Eumenides*). In the second half the resemblances to satyr drama become apparent. The two halves of the action are bridged by the character of Heracles. Admetus, who does not want to violate the laws of hospitality, welcomes the hero into his house but does not tell him of Alcestis's self-sacrifice (476ff.). The rescue plot familiar from satyr drama is initiated when, after the mourners have left the stage, Heracles learns the real reason for Admetus's suffering. It is in Heracles' nature to help those in distress, and so he frees Alcestis from the clutches of Death. Thus the villain is cheated out of his victim (another motif from satyr drama).

This happy ending, which counterbalances the pathos of the farewell scene and mourning scene with which the first half ends, has already been foretold by Apollo in the prologue. In his later plays Euripides makes frequent use of this device, which found its way into the compositional repertory of New Comedy. The chief function of the expository prologue in the economy of the play is to apprise the audience of the background against which the action of the play is to be understood. Because the ending is also anticipated, the audience's attention is directed to the *manner* in which the action is guided to its predetermined end. What excites the audience is the dramatic irony, the incongruity between what it knows in advance and the imperfect knowledge of the dramatis personae. By announcing in the prologue the complications and perils that the characters will have to face because of their deficient knowledge, Euripides succeeds in "evoking the spectator's compassion for the characters even when these characters themselves believe that they hardly deserve that compassion" (G. E. Lessing, *Hamburg Dramaturgy,* Essay 49).

In the prologue of *Alcestis* Apollo says that he has persuaded the Fates to postpone the appointed death of Admetus, at whose court the god served for one year as a cowherd to atone for having killed the Cyclopes. But there is one condition: Admetus will be spared only if another is found to die in his stead. His wife, Alcestis, has volunteered, and this day is to be her last. In his clash with Death, Apollo prophesies that all will end happily in spite of Death's defiance (64–71). The conflict between the chthonic and Olympian gods, which pervades Aeschylus's *Eumenides,* is settled here in the lighthearted manner of comedy. Anticipating that Apollo will once again encroach on his domain and thereby diminish his honor, Death is furious, while his adversary, the Olympian god, remains condescending, derisive, and yet imperious.

What made Euripides' play different from Phrynichus's and Aeschylus's versions of the story, which have not been preserved, was, perhaps, the fact that it did not focus on Alcestis's tragic decision to die for her husband. Instead, that decision has been made years before the beginning of the action, which instead focuses on her death after years of marriage. This change of focus allowed Euripides to dramatize in all its ramifications the predicament of two people confronting Death, who is all the more imposing because, contrary to the conventions of the Attic theater, he is represented onstage. The servant's report, from which the expectant chorus learns of what has transpired in the palace (141ff.), and the farewell scene, in which

Alcestis parts with her husband and children, reveal events as seen from a woman's perspective. Like Deianeira in Sophocles' *Trachinian Women*, Alcestis must give up her sphere of interest, the household which she manages as Admetus's wife, and she requests that no one take her place after she has died. Reminding her husband of what she is sacrificing for his sake, she makes him promise not to take another woman into his house as a stepmother to her children. Alcestis's sense of duty contributes to the poignancy of the farewell scene. She is concerned to ensure—through what is virtually a contract—that after her death no one should encroach on the domestic sphere for which she has been responsible during her life.

Only after the death of Alcestis does Admetus learn the true price of his salvation. He understands too late (940) that life without his beloved wife has no meaning. His suffering is not merely personal: it affects his whole house. Whereas Alcestis, like most Athenian women of the fifth century, sees to the ordering of affairs within the house, Admetus fears that the reputation of the house may be compromised from without. His wife's self-sacrifice, he imagines, will bring reproach upon him; every stranger will accuse him of being a coward (954ff.). The social obligation, which Admetus, as host to Heracles, feels himself bound to fulfill, is brought out clearly in two scenes. Because he wants neither to fail in the duty of hospitality nor to be denounced as a bad host (553ff.), Admetus entertains Heracles generously in his house and, despite his promise to Alcestis (328ff.), takes in the veiled woman whom Heracles, insisting on his prerogative as guest, places in his care until he should return from his next adventure. Admetus, of course, has no idea that Heracles is in fact giving him his own wife. Only when Admetus, bowing to his obligation and violating his promise to Alcestis, escorts the woman into the house does Heracles lift her veil and restore her to her husband.

To Admetus's mind, the social obligation (the duty of

hospitality) outweighs his solemn promise to his wife. Twice, within a very short period, he must break that promise. He admits into his house both a guest and a strange woman. Admetus does not honor the request that Alcestis regards, from a woman's perspective, as fitting and just compensation for her sacrifice (302) because, for him, the public obligation is prior to the private one. As often in Euripides, the happy, fairytale ending conceals the dilemma. In fact the opposing positions of man and woman in this play cannot be reconciled.

In his first play, *Daughters of Pelias* (455), Euripides had already dealt with one part of the story of Jason and Medea. Twenty-four years later, in 431, he returned to the figure of Medea. Although this play was very popular in later centuries, being revived so frequently that it came to be interspersed with histrionic interpolations (see p. 4), it did not bring Euripides victory at the time of its first production; on that occasion, in fact, Euripides placed only third behind Sophocles and Euphorion, the son of Aeschylus, who were awarded the second and first prizes, respectively.

Medea is the central figure of the play. In this respect she may be compared with Sophocles' protagonists. Like Oedipus, she dominates the dramatic action from beginning to end, as is apparent even from the epitome prefixed to the play by an anonymous grammarian:

Jason comes to Corinth, bringing Medea with him, and becomes engaged to Glauce, daughter of Creon, king of the Corinthians. Facing banishment from Corinth by Creon, Medea appeals to him for one day's respite and obtains it. In return for this favor she sends gifts to Glauce through her children, a robe and a garland of gold, and Glauce is destroyed when she puts them on. Creon embraces his daughter and perishes too. Medea kills her own children and, borne on a chariot of winged serpents that she received from

Helius, flees to Athens, where she marries Aegeus, son of Pandion.

The series of scenes in which Medea contrives her revenge on Jason, who has acquiesced in her expulsion from Corinth, is fraught with mounting tension. First her desperate cries are heard offstage (96ff.). From the moment of her entrance she can think of nothing but revenge; she considers only how she might punish Jason for his shameless betrayal (260ff.). Creon enters to inform Medea that he is banishing her from Corinth but is moved by her flattery to grant her a single day's grace (271ff.). Thus, she is compelled to carry out her plan of revenge within this short period (401–9). But the execution of her plan is interrupted by the interview of Jason with his former wife, which serves to characterize Jason. He is a typical aristocrat concerned primarily for his own social standing and his own advantage, who, in a flimsy argument, represents his betrayal as a benefaction to Medea and the children and tries to play down the contributions that she has made to his success. Aegeus, king of Athens, now arrives in Corinth (663ff.). He has suffered from sterility and is on his way to Delphi to consult the oracle. Medea realizes that he is just what she needs in order to carry out her plan, and with the promise of a remedy, she induces him to grant her sanctuary in Athens. Having secured his pledge, she elaborates how she will get at Jason by utterly destroying his "house" (772–97):

> Now I will tell you my entire plan. Do you hear my words, not to your pleasure. I will send one of my servants to ask Jason to come and see me. When he comes I will speak soft words to him, telling him that I agree with him: the marriage into the ruling house that he, my betrayer, is considering is for the best, being both expedient and well thought out. And I will ask that my children be allowed to remain. I would not leave them in a hostile land to be mocked by my enemies.

Instead, with their help, I intend guilefully to kill the
daughter of the king. For I will send my children with
gifts in their hands, bringing to the bride a delicate
robe and a garland of beaten gold, petitioning that they
may not be made to flee this land. And if she takes
these ornaments and puts them on her skin, the girl,
and whoever touches her, will die in agony. With such
potent poisons will I anoint the gifts. Now, however, I
broach another subject. I wail at the thought of what a
terrible deed I must now undertake! For I will slay my
children. No one will be able to take them from me!
Having demolished Jason's entire house, I will depart
from this land, fleeing the consequences of my dearest
children's murder, since it is a most unholy deed that
I dare to do. And yet I must do it. For, my friends, I cannot tolerate being mocked by my enemies.

The intrigue is carried out in the second part of the play
(764–1419). In the knowledge that Aegeus has promised
her asylum provided that she reaches Athens without his
aid, she makes a "deception speech," leading Jason to
believe that she is going to submit after all. She succeeds
in persuading him to let the children go ahead with the
deadly gifts to Creon's daughter, Creusa. After the gifts
have worked the destruction of both Creusa and Creon,
she consummates her revenge by taking the lives of her
own two children.

The figure of Medea may be compared to the hero of
Sophocles' *Ajax*. Like Ajax, Medea fears for her reputation; she is afraid of becoming a laughingstock because of
the disgrace that Jason has brought upon her (383, 404,
797, 1049, 1355). Just as in *Ajax* the hero's desperate act
jeopardizes the social standing, indeed the lives, of his
dependents Tecmessa, Eurysaces, Teucer, and the chorus,
so in *Medea* the nurse already voices her concern for her
mistress's children in the prologue (36, 90), in which
Medea's screams are heard (just as Ajax's screams are

heard in the prologue of Sophocles' play), and has them brought to safety (just as Tecmessa protects her son Eurysaces in *Ajax*). The one day's grace is significant in both plays; like Ajax, Medea has recourse to a deception speech. But apart from these similarities, there are two important differences that make *Medea* unique. Whereas in *Ajax* Tecmessa is a foil to the tragic hero, an ordinary person who, in her clashes with him, represents norms of behavior against which his convictions and motives stand out all the more sharply, such a foil to Medea is lacking in Euripides' play. The conflict of emotions, the struggle between a mother's love for her children and an injured spouse's unquenchable thirst for revenge, takes place within a single personality. Gazing into her children's eyes, she fights this battle within herself (1042–52):

> Alas! What am I to do? My heart left me, women, when I saw my children's bright faces. I couldn't do it. Away with my former plans! I will take my children with me from this land. Why should I hurt their father by their suffering and bring upon myself twice as much suffering? I can't do it. Away with my former plans! And yet what is the matter with me? Do I want to let my enemies go unpunished and be mocked? I must venture this thing. What a coward I am even to admit these soft arguments to my mind.

The other essential difference between Medea and Ajax is that Medea succeeds in taking her revenge, while Ajax does not. Like a deus ex machina, she vanishes to Athens on Helius's chariot, after establishing, again like a god, an expiatory cult for her children and foretelling Jason's death (1378–88). This ending, criticized by Aristotle (*Poetics* 1454a 37) as an inorganic appendage, is simply the logical outcome of the game that the poet has been playing with the feelings of the audience. If the image of a woman abandoned by her husband and without the privileges of citizenship has hitherto elicted the audience's compassion, that image is shattered when she commits the inhuman act of murder. If the murder of the children is, as is generally believed, an innovation on the part of Euripides, it probably came as a horrible surprise to the audience. Its compassion is transmuted into revulsion. By making Medea virtually divine at the end of the play, Euripides removes her entirely from the human sphere, from human norms and values. The heroine is mistress of her own destiny; she does not have to yield to a retributive oracle as does the humiliated Jason, but is able to go to Athens unimpeded by virtue of her agreement with Aegeus. But what will her life be like after she has slain her own children? This question exposes the dubiousness, the fragility, of Medea's triumph.

In 428, a few years after his first treatment of the story of Phaedra and Hippolytus in *Hippolytus Veiling Himself*, Euripides wrote a second version of the myth, which took first prize. We may reasonably assume that in the first *Hippolytus* it was Phaedra herself who made improper suggestions to her stepson, whereupon he covered his head in shame (whence the adjunct "Veiling Himself"). Seneca's *Phaedra* is based largely on this version. Phaedra's blatant attempt to seduce her stepson is said to have offended the Athenians. Therefore, after the failure of the first play, according to the grammarian in his hypothesis, Euripides wrote a second play, omitting whatever had been "indecent and censurable" in the first.

Unlike *Medea, Hippolytus* lacks a dominant character. The action neither receives its vital impulse from, nor is centered on, a single person. Rather, the relationships between the nurse, Phaedra, Hippolytus, and Theseus, as well as the opposition of the two goddesses, Aphrodite in the prologue and Artemis in the exodos, create a field of opposing forces in which the dramatic events take their fateful course.

It has often been maintained that if one were to remove the gods from *Hippolytus* its action would lose nothing of its logical consistency. It can be shown, however, that it is just this divine frame that imparts meaning to the intentions and actions of the characters in this play.

Hippolytus, Theseus, Phaedra, and the nurse embody four different views of life. None of these characters, however, is capable of resisting the unpredictable power of sexual love. As they repeatedly assert, both Hippolytus and Phaedra endeavor to live in accordance with the aristocratic ideal of *sōphrosynē*, the virtue of sensible, self-controlled living. When her passion, which she holds to be pernicious and disgraceful, proves stronger than her sōphrosynē, Phaedra feels that she must kill herself to preserve both her own good reputation (*kleos*) as the king's wife and that of Theseus's house (398ff., 715ff.). At the same time she wants to avenge herself on her unapproachable stepson (725–31): "Before this day is over I will please Aphrodite, my destroyer, by leaving this life. Bitter is the love whose victim I will be. Yet in dying I will make another suffer, in order that he may know not to gloat over my suffering. Having shared in my sickness, he will learn sōphrosynē." Hippolytus's sōphrosynē, of which he boasts from the beginning, is shown in the course of the play to be just the opposite: his one-sided veneration of Artemis and the contempt he shows for the goddess of love show up his claim to sōphrosynē as hubristic. For he lacks the two basic qualities presupposed by this virtue: insight into his own nature and an avoidance of extremes.

In the fifth century sōphrosynē was an oligarchic slogan. Hippolytus's claim, then, suggested to the audience that his political outlook was oligarchic. His character thus took on a political dimension. Euripides predisposed his democratic audience against Hippolytus. Not only does Euripides make Hippolytus claim to have put sōphrosynē into practice; he also, in the prologue, represents him as a passionate hunter. Hunting was an aristocratic pastime. As a typical aristocrat Hippolytus would not have elicited much sympathy from the audience. He even justifies his elitist position openly before the people, and his tone is unmistakably condescending (983ff.). Yet if Hippolytus has hitherto been beyond the pale of the audience's sympathy, the gap between them is bridged at the end of the play. Such last-minute conciliation of audience and tragic hero is typically Euripidean. Tormented by pain and about to die, Hippolytus is reconciled with his father and forgives him (1446ff.). At last the audience is able to feel for the hero.

The network of human relations is fixed within the framework of divine conflict. In the prologue Aphrodite says that she will punish Hippolytus, not for his immoderate veneration of Artemis, but for the contempt with which she herself has been treated by him. She praises the excellence of Phaedra's character, but maintains that, if divine revenge is to be effected, Theseus's wife must die. In the exodos Artemis announces to the grieving father and the dying son that she will not let Hippolytus's death go unavenged, but with her arrows will lay low whoever is dearest to Aphrodite (1420–22). Thus, the two goddesses, despite the oppositions which they represent, are similar in the end. Each is inhumanely cruel in defending her domain, her honor (*timē*), against the other. Mortals are mere instruments in the divine power struggle. Their thoughts and actions are doomed to failure, turn into the opposite of what they intended, and prove futile and meaningless. Yet the immediate cause of the gods' cruelty is not the arbitrary will of divinity, but the misguided conduct, the hubris of mortals. In this respect the theology of Euripides' *Hippolytus* approaches Aeschylean theodicy.

The Cruelty of the Gods and the Triumph of Human Kindness: *Heracles*

In *Heracles* Euripides developed further the ideas about gods and mortals that he had explored some twelve years earlier in *Hippolytus*.

While Heracles is performing the last of the labors

imposed on him by Eurystheus, the fetching of the hound
Cerberus from Hades, a certain Lycus has seized power in
Thebes and is threatening to kill the hero's family: his old
"stepfather" Amphitryon, his wife Megara, and his children. Heracles returns just in time to kill the usurper
(1–814). Hardly has the chorus of old Thebans begun to
sing a song of jubilation when Iris, the messenger of the
gods, and Lyssa, the goddess of madness, appear. The old
men react to their epiphany with cries of horror. The goddesses have been sent by Hera to derange Heracles' senses
and drive him to kill his children (815ff.). The chorus
strikes up a lament, which is cut short by Amphitryon's
shrieks from within the house. A servant enters to inform
the old men of a dreadful turn of events. Heracles, believing that he was destroying Eurystheus and his sons, has
slaughtered his own wife and children. He would also have
killed his father, the servant reports, were it not for the
intervention of Athena, who knocked him senseless with
a stone. He is wheeled out on the ekkyklēma, regains con-
sciousness, and learns the horrible truth from his father.
Only Theseus, who had sought to help his friend destroy
the usurper, is able to prevent him from taking his own life
by promising him asylum and expiation in Athens.

As this short paraphrase shows, the play falls into two
parts. In the first (1–814), the suspense builds until the
hero returns and rescues his family; in the second, which
begins with the epiphany of Iris and Lyssa, the hero's for-
tunes take a startling turn. The second half is not, however, an inorganic appendage; rather, in both structure and
content it rounds off, and is a necessary consequence of,
the preceding action.

The dramatic structure of *Heracles* is marked by constant vacillation between the extremes of hope and despair.
Amphitryon condemns Zeus (339–47), charging that the
god could steal into his wife Alcmena's bed and beget Heracles, but now no longer cares about his son and family. At
first his accusations appear to be refuted by the fact of Heracles' return. But no sooner do the old men of the chorus,

for whom Lycus's undoing proves that "justice is still dear
to the gods," finish singing of Heracles' triumph (810–14)
than they cry out in horror at the epiphany of Iris and
Lyssa (815–17). The chorus leader's subsequent denunciation of Zeus (1086f.) recalls Amphitryon's outcry (339ff.).

   The play owes its unity above all to the figure of Heracles, who remains at its center from beginning to end:
around him revolve, in the first half, the hopes of all the
other characters; his actions and his suffering determine
the course of the second half. As in Sophocles' *Trachinian
Women*, the lives of all the other characters depend on the
hero. The superhuman stature of the Sophoclean Heracles
predisposes the audience to be indifferent to his suffering;
his Euripidean counterpart, by contrast, is portrayed from
the outset as a "family man": having accomplished his
labors, he comes home to a family that loves him dearly,
and he, for his part, loves his wife and children and promises to keep them from harm (622–36):

> Come, children, follow your father into the house.
> You're happier now to be going in than you were when
> you first came out, aren't you? But take courage, and
> don't let those tears fall from your eyes any longer.
> Dear wife, pull yourself together, stop trembling, and
> let go of my robes, all of you! For I have no wings and
> do not wish to flee from those whom I love. Ha! They
> will not let go, but cling all the more tightly to my
> clothes! You really were on a razor's edge, weren't you,
> little ones? Well, I'll take these little boats myself and
> lead them by the hand. Like a big ship I'll tow them.
> I'll not neglect my children. The affairs of mortals are
> the same in this respect: everyone, no matter what
> his standing, loves his child. In wealth, it is true, peo-
> ple are different: some have it, others do not. Yet they
> all love their children.

Heracles is portrayed not as an aloof, superhuman demigod but as a mortal man whose emotions everyone can

readily understand—we may even find him congenial. He elicits not our admiration but our compassion. Because we feel for him, the horror with which we react to his sudden and unexpected change of fortune is all the more intense. Hera has compelled him to undertake twelve all but impossible labors simply because he was Alcmena's child by Zeus and not her own. Having endured all these toils and shown himself to be humanity's greatest benefactor, he is now thrust by the goddess into the worst calamity imaginable. Faced with her grim mission, even Lyssa is reluctant to obey Hera's commands (849–54): "This man, against whose house you are sending me, is not without distinction either on earth or among the gods. He has civilized a remote land and a savage sea, and he alone restored the honors of the gods when they were neglected by impious men. So I do not advise you to devise great suffering for him."

The theology of *Heracles* is decidedly more radical than that of *Hippolytus*. Hippolytus is destroyed by his hubris, his lack of reverence for Aphrodite. As an aristocrat who regards the people with contempt (986ff.), he can hardly garner the audience's sympathy, at least not until the exodos. Aphrodite's cruelty was aroused by his misconduct, and, as Artemis foretells in the exodos, that cruelty will bring cruel requital in its train. Not so in *Heracles:* in this play Hera's cruelty arises from her jealousy, from her quarrel with her husband. In these conflicts mortals become the playthings of blind, irrational forces; they are placed within a mechanism whose working they cannot understand and from which there is no escape. Mortal views of the nature of the gods always turn out to be wrong: thus, the hopeful words of the chorus (810–14) or the argument, made by Heracles in answer to Theseus, that the gods are not motivated by passion (1341ff.). Amphitryon's despairing indictment of Zeus (339ff.) is borne out in the course of the play as Heracles' explanation is not.

The only source of hope in this cruel, irrational, indeed absurd world is to be found not in the gods but in mortals themselves: Heracles' greatness lies in the fact that he does not kill himself in order to avoid disgrace, like the hero of Sophocles' *Ajax*, but chooses to go on living with the burden of what he has done.

Just as *Hippolytus* ends not with a vow of revenge by Artemis but with the reconciliation of father and son, so *Heracles* closes with an image of humanity. Heracles leaves the stage supported by his friend Theseus, who has been able to divert him from his suicidal thoughts and now offers him, the outcast, asylum in Athens. In this world, for all its absurdity, friendship and human kindness prevail.

The Hero as Common Citizen: *Electra*

We have seen how, in *Heracles*, Euripides portrays the son of Zeus and Alcmena as a loving father and in this way enlists the audience's sympathy on the side of the tragic hero. This tendency to reduce the tragic hero to the status of an average citizen is even more evident in *Electra*, which was produced a few years before *Heracles*.

Euripides altered the traditional story by introducing Electra, in the prologue, as the wife of an impoverished aristocrat living in the country and working the soil with his own hands. Aegisthus had arranged the marriage in order that his stepdaughter, her husband, and their descendants might be powerless to oppose him. The play has its basis in everyday life. Electra typifies the capable and self-respecting fifth-century Athenian woman: she draws water from the public fountain (54ff.); on the approach of strange men (Orestes and Pylades), she is inclined to withdraw into the house (215–19) and is scolded by her spouse when he finds her talking to the strangers (341–44); she takes great pains to be duly hospitable towards the guests, whom her husband has invited into their cottage (404ff.). The audience can recognize its own problems, worries, and values in what is represented on the stage.

In the first part of the play (1–595), Euripides disposes his audience to identify with these "ordinary" characters; in the second (596–1171), in which Agamemnon's children plan and execute their acts of vengeance, even the victims of Orestes' and Electra's intrigue are represented, contrary to the audience's expectations, as ordinary people. Aegisthus is a jovial host who unsuspectingly invites his guests to a sacrificial feast only to have a cleaver plunged into his back by Orestes (774ff.). Clytemnestra has long since recognized that the murder of Agamemnon was unjust (1105–10). She forgives her daughter for hating her, since she knows that Electra was very fond of her father (1102–4). From the moment of her entrance, Clytemnestra is concerned about her child (1007). Indeed, Euripides draws attention to her maternal side. She addresses Electra as her "child" (1057, 1106, 1123), in sharp contrast to her Sophoclean counterpart, who calls her daughter a "shameless brat" (622).

By characterizing Clytemnestra as woman whose emotions and actions everyone can understand, Euripides engages the audience's sympathy for her. When doubts suddenly well up in Orestes himself (962ff.), who a moment ago was still intent on revenge, and when both brother and sister collapse helplessly after the deed has been accomplished (1177ff.), the audience's disposition towards them can only be more sympathetic.

Euripides makes the matricide seem all the more cruel by treating the curse on the descendants of Atreus, so prominent in Aeschylus's *Oresteia,* only peripherally (1306f.), and by relegating Apollo's oracle to the background. The god's command does not have the menacing quality that it has in Aeschylus. Instead, Electra is driven by her unremitting hatred of Aegisthus and her mother. Her hatred stems both from her father's murder and from the loss of dignity that she has suffered at the hands of her father's murderers. She openly displays that loss by voluntarily doing the work of an ordinary woman.

The deus ex machina scene, in which Castor and Polydeuces disentangle the knots of the story, restoring order to the chaos that mortals have left behind, recalls *Heracles*. The Dioscuri find fault with Apollo for having ordered the matricide (1245f., 1302). Their criticism shows that mortals are caught within a web of unfathomable forces: even the instructions of the Delphic god are not infallible, but can be just as reckless and imprudent (cf. 1245f.) as human actions.

The Transvaluation of Heroism and the Loss of Humanity: *Phoenician Women — Orestes — Iphigeneia at Aulis*

Two recurrent themes in *Phoenician Women* and *Orestes* are the subversion of heroic values and the erosion of human feeling. Both plays were produced at a time when Athenian politics, both foreign and domestic, were fraught with tension. In the aftermath of the devastating failure of the Sicilian expedition, a board of ten *probouloi* was established (413) that in some way restricted the organs of democratic government. Some Athenians, it seems, blamed the catastrophe in Sicily on the democracy. Then, in 411, oligarchic extremists staged a coup. It was not until about a year later, in 410, that the radical democracy was restored. During these restless years, no one knew where his neighbor stood; Athenians became uncertain about the values and norms that had formed the basis of their sociopolitical lives. At the same time, the crisis was the ideal breeding ground for unscrupulous politicians interested in making a career for themselves and in acquiring power. Such were Phrynichus and Theramenes, and, in particular, Alcibiades. After he was recalled from his command in Sicily because of his alleged involvement in the mutilation of the herms and in the profanation of the mysteries, Alcibiades went over to Sparta, where he did everything he could to harm Athens (he advised the Spartans to capture the Attic border fortress Decelea, for example). Finally, when things got too hot for him there, he went to the court of the Persian satrap of Sardis, Tissaphernes, from which, after a short time, he renewed contact with the oligarchs in Athens. In the end, though, he rejoined the democrats.

In his account of the Peloponnesian War, Thucydides analyzes, in a passage known as the "Pathology," the deterioration of political conduct and the transvaluation of political ideas — accepted values were largely repudiated — that characterized this period not only in Athens but in nearly all the cities of war-torn Greece (3.82). It is against this background that one must read Euripides' *Phoenician Women* and *Orestes* as well as Sophocles' *Philoctetes:*

So, as strife followed strife from city to city, the later outbreaks, by knowledge of what had gone before, were marked by ever increasing novelty of plan, shown both in the ingenuity of attack and in the enormity of revenge. The customary meanings of words were changed as men claimed the right to use them as they would to suit their actions: an unreasoning daring was called courage and loyalty to party, a prudent delay specious cowardice; moderation and self-control came to be reckoned but the cloak of timidity, to have an understanding of the whole to be everywhere unwilling to act. A capricious cunning was added to the brave man's portion; to deliberate for long so as to avoid mistakes was supposed a well-thought excuse for avoiding action. So the man who quarrelled was always believed, his opponent always suspect. If a man plotted and succeeded, he was intelligent; if he suspected a plot he was even cleverer; and one who took care so that neither plot nor suspicion be needed was a subverter of his party and intimidated by the other side. Applause, in a word, went to one who got in first with some evil act, and to him who cheered on another to attempt some crime that he was not thinking of. Kinship became more foreign than party, for party friends were readier for action without demur; for such associations were formed not for the sake of mutual aid under the existing laws, but for gain by illegal means. Good faith between the members of a party was secured not by the sanction of divine law so much as by partnership in crime; and as for fair offers from opponents, they were received only with precautionary *action* by the stronger party, not with candor and generosity. A man thought more of avenging an injury than of having no injury to avenge. When sworn treaties *were* agreed to, the oaths taken stood for a brief time while each party was in difficulties and had no help from outside; but in a moment, the man who plucked up courage first when he saw his enemy off his guard was more delighted with his revenge because of the good faith broken than he would have been with an open fight—the safety of the deed was considered and, because he had won by a trick, he got laurels for his intelligence. At such times most men are readily called either, if they are knaves, clever, or fools if they are honest, and they are ashamed of the latter and glory in the former.

The cause of it all was love of power to gratify greed and personal ambition; from that came the eagerness to quarrel which appeared once strife had begun. (Trans. A. W. Gomme, *A Historical Commentary on Thucydides*, 5 vols. [Oxford, 1956] 2:384.)

In *Phoenician Women* Euripides returns to the subject of Aeschylus's *Seven against Thebes*, inspired, perhaps, by a revival of that play. Euripides' play differs from that of Aeschylus in four crucial respects. First, Euripides' Eteocles seems morally inferior to his Aeschylean counterpart. His motives for defending the city are ignoble; in fact, his only object is to remain in power, in spite of his agreement with Polyneices. At first Polyneices' claim is presented as more just than that of Eteocles, because the latter has breached their agreement. In the event, however, his heroic standing is subverted by an insatiable will to power. Related to the characterization of the two brothers and to the representation of their respective claims is the second conspicuous difference. The chorus consists not of citizens of war-stricken Thebes but of Phoenician maidens who happen to be passing through the city. They witness the action as disinterested observers. Consequently, the civic body, which is immediately affected by the threat of civil conflict, and the public interest, which is represented in Aeschylus's play by the chorus of Theban women, are in effect cut out of the picture, so that our attention is fixed on the private quarrel between the brothers. The third difference is Jocasta's unsuccessful attempt to conciliate her sons. As the violence escalates, the voice that pleads for conciliation goes unheard. Fourth, there is the figure of Creon's son, Menoeceus. An invention of the poet, he is the only ray of light in this otherwise dark and hopeless confusion. Menoeceus gives up his life voluntarily to save the city, despite the vehement resistance of his father, who would sooner sacrifice the city than his son.

A few years later, Euripides once again made the expiatory death of a young person the focal point of one of his plays. In the posthumously produced *Iphigeneia at Aulis*, Agamemnon's daughter voluntarily gives up her life for the sake of all Greeks. By resolving to accept and even appropriate the inevitable, Iphigeneia, like Polyxena in *Hecuba* (see p. 114), makes the "heroism" of an Achilleus or Agamemnon seem all the more precarious and questionable.

Also favorably drawn is the other young person in *Phoenician Women*, Antigone. When we meet her at the beginning of the play, she is an ordinary young woman leading the life of sequestration considered appropriate for her age and sex in Athens at that time. In the course of the action, however, her character becomes increasingly resolute. She foregoes her private happiness, her marriage to Haemon, to accompany her blind father into exile, and declares that she will discharge her duty as the next of kin and bury Polyneices at all costs, even if it entails giving up her own life.

Thus, two young individuals—Menoeceus, the savior of the polis, and Antigone, the upholder of familial and religious duty—stand out as positive figures against the background of a society plunged into chaos by hate and lust for power.

Produced in 408, a few years after *Phoenician Women*, *Orestes* is almost wholly devoid of the light that shines through the gloom of power politics in the earlier play. The naive, kind-hearted Hermione is the only glimmer, and she is a minor figure. Among literary critics from antiquity to the present, *Orestes* has won little acclaim. In his *Poetics* (1454a 29, 1461b 21f.) Aristotle finds fault with the poet for drawing Menelaus's character morally worse than necessary. In his introduction to *Orestes*, Aristophanes of Byzantium says that its ending would be better suited to a comedy. Following Aristotle, Aristophanes dismisses its characters, with the exception of Pylades, as morally inferior, though he does commend its theatrical effectiveness. In his *Lectures on Literature* A. W. Schlegel calls the play a *Spektakelstück*—mere spectacle.

Orestes begins six days after the murder of Clytemnestra and Aegisthus. The situation in which Orestes and Electra find themselves corresponds to their predicament in *Electra* before the appearance of the Dioscuri (1177ff.). Electra, who has seen her brother tormented by fits of madness (36–37), censures Apollo for having given Orestes the oracular mandate to kill his mother (28–32). To Orestes' inner burden of remorse is now added an outer pressure: imminent condemnation by the Argive citizenry (46ff.).

Henceforth Orestes and Electra look to their uncle Menelaus, who has just returned from Troy after many wander-
ings, as their last hope. But Menelaus selfishly refuses to
help them. Pylades rouses them from their despair at having been betrayed by their uncle (729ff.). He advises
Orestes to make his case before the assembly of the Argive
people. When this attempt fails (844ff.), Pylades suggests
that, since Orestes must die in any event, he at least do so
with honor. To this end he proposes that they make his
detested uncle suffer by murdering his wife Helen (1105).
At this point Electra conceives the idea of kidnapping
Menelaus's daughter Hermione and thus compelling Menelaus to ransom his child by lending his assistance (1177f.).
Heroism has been subordinated to the will to live.

Orestes and Pylades see the murder of an innocent, cred-
ulous, and kindhearted girl as act of heroism. Thus, their
"heroism" has been subverted. The play enacts the transvaluation of the traditional concept. If the audience has
sympathized with the avengers up to this point, its sympathy now changes to revulsion.

Helen suddenly disappears, and the plan to kill her
must be abandoned. The kidnapping of Hermione, however, comes off successfully. Orestes appears on the roof of
the palace and tells Menelaus that, unless he agrees to
help, his daughter will die. The situation has changed dras-
tically since the two first met (385ff.): now it is Orestes
who has the upper hand and is making threats, whereas
Menelaus is the weaker and sees that he is at a disadvan-
tage (1617). Even after Menelaus has yielded, Orestes
orders Electra to set the palace on fire (this inconsistency
has occasioned much scholarly debate). At this highly sus-
penseful moment the god Apollo appears ex machina and
restores order (1625ff.).

This ending and, above all, the characterization and
motivation of the dramatis personae, which have so often
been criticized, should be seen against the background of
the sociopolitical conditions in Athens after the cata-

strophic failure of the Sicilian expedition as described in the "Pathology" of Thucydides.

Orestes, Pylades, and Electra form a secret society which they themselves call a *hetaireia* ('political club,' 804, 1072, 1079), a political catchword of the day. These three will stop at nothing to achieve their aims. They go so far as to contemplate murdering an innocent and defenseless person and regard the assassination as an act of heroism. Their adversary, the power-hungry and cunning Menelaus, considers only his own advantage. He is characterized as a student of the sophists, a man with a keen eye for what is expedient in any situation. Tyndareus represents the aristocratic faction; he is a politician of the old school. Typical in this respect are his ties to the popular assembly, to which the people flock more to be entertained by the speaker than to assess the soundness of his arguments.

The characters in the dramatic performance reflect the reality of everyday life in Athens, which towards the end of the Peloponnesian War was no longer intelligible by traditional standards. The gloomy outlook of *Orestes* is not unlike that of Sophocles' *Philoctetes*, which was produced one year earlier. In both plays human actions lead to chaos—in Sophocles because mortal knowledge is insufficient, in Euripides because mortals are hateful, violent, and brutal. Order is restored only by a deus ex machina. Consumed by hate, Orestes orders that the palace be set ablaze even after he has brought Menelaus to his knees. For, as Thucydides writes, revenge was considered more important than self-preservation.

By the time Apollo arrives ex machina to force the action back into congruity with the outcome predetermined by the myth, the gap between the chaos of human action and the order restored by divinity has become too abrupt for the audience to mistake the utter unreality of the play's ending. Euripides is suggesting that, while such a happy ending is possible in the theater, it is not in everyday life. In reality, as Euripides' contemporary Thucydides writes, it is lust for power, greed, ambition, and rash impetuosity that prevail.

War and Its Aftermath:
Hecuba—Trojan Women

If, as we have seen in the light of Thucydides' analysis of the effects of civil conflict (3.82), *Phoenician Women* and *Orestes* gave expression, through the vehicle of myth, to the hopelessness, dissension, and political intrigue that plagued Athens in the years following the calamity in Sicily. *Hecuba* and *Trojan Women* dramatized the aftermath of war. Both plays, to be sure, reflected the woeful experiences of the Peloponnesian War (*Hecuba* was produced during the Archidamian War, *Trojan Women* on the eve of the Sicilian expedition). Yet it is pointless to look for allusions to particular historical events or even political figures, as some have tried to do, especially in *Trojan Women*. In these plays, as in *Orestes* or *Phoenician Women*, the poet mirrored the emotions, concerns, fears, and patterns of conduct that characterized political life in wartime Athens and, by situating them in mythic contexts and making effective use of theatrical illusion, lent them universal validity.

Hecuba and *Trojan Women*, like Aeschylus's *Persians*, dramatize the aftermath of a devastating defeat as seen from the perspective of the conquered. In these plays Euripides focuses on the misfortunes of the Trojan queen and her family. Hecuba has lost her husband, Priam, her sons, and her daughters. She is pitched from the heights of royal power into the depths of humiliating enslavement.

Let me lie as I have fallen (kindness, if unwelcome, is no kindness, O maidens). I suffer, have suffered, and will yet suffer things that warrant such prostrations. Gods! You are ineffectual allies whom I invoke; but there is something to be said for calling on the gods, whenever one of us encounters misfortunes. First, I wish to sing of my blessings, for thereby I will excite greater pity for my woes. I was a ruler's child and married into a ruler's house, and then I gave birth to preeminent children, no mere number, but the finest of the Phrygians, of whose like no woman—Trojan, Greek, or barbarian—could ever boast. These I have seen fall by the Greek spear; I have shorn these locks at the tombs that contain their corpses; I have wept for Priam, their begetter. I did not hear of his death from others but with my own eyes saw him slaughtered at this household altar, and the city taken. The maidens whom I raised to be a choice honor for bridegrooms, I raised, in the event, for strangers; they were taken from my hands. There is no hope that I will ever be seen by them, much less that I will ever see them myself. Finally, what is the coping stone of my wretched woes, I will arrive in Greece an old slave woman. They will subject me to tasks least suited to this old age of mine: as a servant I will either keep the keys to the doors—I, who brought forth Hector!—or bake bread; for my wrinkled back I will have, instead of royal mattresses, a bed on the ground; I will wear tattered rags over my tattered skin, rags disgraceful for the prosperous to possess. Alas, wretched me, what I have suffered, and will yet suffer, because of one marriage of one woman! O child, O Cassandra, you who join with the gods in Dionysiac revelry, amid what calamities did you lose your virginity! And you, O wretched one, Polyxena, where are you? No offspring, no son or daughter, out of all my many children, can help wretched me. Why, then, O maidens, are you lifting me up? What are your hopes? Guide my foot, once dainty in Troy, but now a slave; convey me to my pallet on the ground and my pillow of rock, in order that I may fall down and die, worn away with tears. Do not consider any of the fortunate to be truly happy until he is dead. (Hecuba's monologue, *Trojan Women* 466–510)

The cruel victor has snatched away all hope from the conquered. In *Hecuba* Priam's wife must first give up her daughter Polyxena to be sacrificed at Achilles' tomb; she then learns that her youngest son, Polydorus, has been murdered out of greed by the Thracian king Polymestor, to whose protection she had entrusted the young prince for the duration of the war. In *Trojan Women*, Hector's little son Astyanax, the Trojans' last hope (702ff.), is torn from the arms of his mother, Andromache, and hurled to his death from a tower, because the Greeks regard any offspring of Hector as a potential threat (709ff.).

If both plays dramatize the suffering of the vanquished, they also point to the precariousness of triumph. It is suggested or even demonstrated on the stage that the victor who gives way to the exaltation of the moment and commits acts of hubris is dancing on the brink of ruin. Odysseus, who is delegated by the Greek army to conduct Polyxena to the tomb of Achilles, where the hero's ghost has demanded that she be sacrificed, singlemindedly carries out his mission, callously rejecting the pleas of her mother Hecuba (*Hecuba* 218ff.); but he will wander for ten years before he sees his home in Ithaca. Polymestor is lured by Hecuba, who pretends to have riches for his safekeeping, into a Trojan tent, where she murders his sons and puts out his eyes. The final words of the prologue of *Trojan Women*, which are spoken by the god Poseidon as he gazes on the destroyed city, convey the moral lesson of that play: "He is a fool who pillages cities, temples, and tombs, the sanctuaries of the dead. For he makes them desolate only to perish himself afterward" (95–97). To achieve victory the Greeks have dared to commit hubristic acts; they have encroached on the prerogatives and honor (*timē*) of the gods, and must be punished, as Poseidon and

Athena declare in the prologue of *Trojan Women*. The victors' hubris, which is the leading theme of the play from prologue to exodos, itself condemns them. In the end, war does not distinguish between vanquisher and vanquished, between the triumphant and the humbled, but brings suffering and death to all alike.

The Praise of Athens:
Suppliant Women — Children of Heracles — Andromache

In the Introduction it was noted that an essential function of the Great Dionysia was to promote a sense of pride and solidarity in the Athenian people and to put on display before the dependent allies and other non-Athenians the wealth, might, and glory of Athens. This function was served not only by the ceremonies with which the Great Dionysia were inaugurated but also by the plays themselves, in particular those which had as a main theme the praise of Athens. In Plato's *Menexenus* Socrates describes the effect that one such laudatory oration (in this case the funeral speech, or *epitaphios*, given annually on the occasion of the festival in honor of the Athenian war dead) might have on the audience (235 a–b):

Speakers praise him [the dead man] for what he has done and what he has not done—that is the beauty of them—and they steal away our souls with their embellished words; in every conceivable form they praise the city; and they praise those who died in war, and all our ancestors who went before us; and they praise ourselves also who are still alive, until I feel quite elevated by their laudations, and I stand listening to their words, Menexenus, and become enchanted by them, and all in a moment I imagine myself to have become a greater and nobler and finer man that I was before. And if, as often happens, there are any foreigners who accompany me to the speech, I become suddenly more dignified in my bearing towards them, and they, so it seems to me, experience a corresponding feeling of admiration at me, and at the greatness of the city, which appears to them, when they are under the influence of the speaker, more wonderful than ever. (Trans. B. Jowett, *The Dialogues of Plato*, 4 vols., 4th ed. [Oxford, 1953] 1:681–82).

Suppliant Women and *Children of Heracles* can be described as dramatic encomia of Athens. In both plays Athens is praised as the champion of the weak. In *Suppliant Women*, the action of which begins where Aeschylus's *Seven against Thebes* left off, Athens, represented by Theseus, defends a mother's right to bury her son, who has fallen in battle; in *Children of Heracles* the sons of Heracles, pursued by Eurystheus, find refuge in Athens.

In both plays Euripides makes use of a plot type known as the "suppliant drama," which is also found in Aeschylus's *Suppliants* and Sophocles' *Oedipus at Colonus:* in need of proctection, the weak find a savior in Athens, which is represented by its "democratic" king, Theseus or Demophon. The attack of the persecutors is repulsed: Athens shows itself to be a secure place of refuge, and the city is praised at great length in hymns of gratitude.

While the praise of Athens is the central theme of *Suppliant Women* and *Children of Heracles* is the praise of Athens, encomiastic inserts are also found in a number of other plays. We may recall Theseus in *Heracles*, who receives the suffering hero in Athens, or the chorus of captive women in *Trojan Women*, who ask that they be allowed to serve as slaves, if serve they must, not in Sparta but in "glorious Athens." As this passage shows (207f.), during the Peloponnesian War denunciation of Sparta went hand in hand with praise of Athens. *Andromache* can therefore be included among the laudatory plays, since it gives us, in the figure of Menelaus, the disagreeable Spartan par excellence.

Palintonos Harmonia: *Iphigeneia*
among the Taurians — *Ion* — *Helen*

Not all of Euripides' late works are as pessimistic as *Phoe-nician Women* or *Orestes*. *Iphigeneia among the Taur-ians*, *Ion*, and *Helen* were also produced after the Sicilian trauma. In these plays myth is interpreted more lightheart-edly, as are the relationships between gods and mortals and between mortals themselves. The poet does this by exper-imenting with traditional plot structures and scene types, and by making use of dramatic irony and surprise effects. All three plays are marked by a *palintonos harmonia*, or harmony of opposites: cheerful elements are combined with a serious basic tenor. Through the vehicle of myth, Euripides shows paradigmatically how mortals are suscep-tible to chance and the intervention of higher powers; how, in their ingenuity, shortsightedness, and temerity, they are able to thwart the designs of the gods (Sophocles' *Philoctetes*, produced at about the same time, comes to mind); and how the gods, for their part, lack insight into mortal emotions, thoughts, and motives.

These plays strike an exotic note. The action of *Iphi-geneia* is laid in the distant, barbarous land of the Taur-ians, that of *Helen* in Egypt. This tendency towards the exotic is also evident in a closely contemporary comedy, Aristophanes' *Birds* (414), and must reflect the audience's taste at that time. In all three plays the poet experiments with the *anagnōrismos*, or recognition scene. He explores the possibilities of dramatic irony: because the audience has been apprised of the true identity of the characters in the prologue, it can follow the action now in amusement, now in suspense, now in alarm.

This irony is at its most intense in *Iphigeneia among the Taurians*. A second oracle of Apollo promises Orestes that the Erinyes will stop hounding him on the condition that he brings the cult statue of Artemis from the land of the Taurians to Athens. He and his companion Pylades are

taken captive by shepherds and brought before the priestess of Artemis. The audience knows that this is Iphigeneia, who was not sacrificed at Aulis but was borne
away by the goddess to the land of the Taurians just as she
was about to be struck by her father's blade. In Iphigeneia's
interview with the two strangers Euripides carries the
anagnōrismos to its extreme (467ff.). The siblings might
recognize each other at any moment; one word would
suffice. But this word, which is keenly anticipated by the
entire audience, is not uttered. Iphigeneia is preparing the
sacrifice that would end her brother's life, when she learns
that the captive Greeks come from the place where she
grew up; she decides to send Pylades to Mycenae with a letter for her brother. Afraid that some mishap might prevent the letter from reaching its destination, she recites
its contents to Pylades in order that he may, if necessary,
convey the message orally (769–93):

Iphigeneia: Deliver a message to Orestes, son of Agamemnon: "Iphigeneia, who was sacrificed at Aulis,
sends these tidings. She lives, but for those who
were there lives no longer . . ."
Orestes: Where is she? Has she died and come back
to life?
Iphigeneia: She is here, you are looking at her. Don't
interrupt me. "Take me away from this barbarous
land, brother, to Argos, before I die, and set me free
from the goddess's sacrifices at which it is my office
to kill strangers . . ."
Orestes: Pylades, what am I to say? Where are we? In
a dream?
Iphigeneia: "Or I will become a curse to your house,
Orestes." I repeat the name that you may not forget
it.
Orestes: O gods!
Iphigeneia: Why do you call on the gods when this
matter is no concern of yours?

Orestes: Never mind. Continue. My thoughts strayed.
Iphigeneia: It may be that he will ask you questions and won't believe you. In that case, tell him: "The goddess Artemis saved me by putting a deer in my place, which my father sacrificed, thinking that his sharp sword was striking me. Then she brought me to this land." That is the letter, that is what is written on the tablets.
Pylades: The oath to which you have bound me is easy to fulfill, and you yourself have sworn excellently. I will not take long in making good the oath I swore. Look! I bear a tablet and deliver it to you, Orestes, from your sister here.
Orestes: I accept it.

Of the three *palintonos harmonia* plays, it was *Ion* that exerted the greatest influence on the development of European drama. For this reason its structure and plot should be treated in greater detail. In the prologue (1–81), Hermes, the messenger of the gods, sets out the events antecedent to the action of the play. Apollo, Hermes explains, raped Creusa, daughter of the Athenian king Erechtheus. She became pregnant, but concealed the fact from her father. Immediately after the child was born, she exposed it in the same cave in which it had been conceived. Thinking that the child was doomed, she placed next to it, as a burial gift, the old jewelry of the Erechtheids — two snakes wrought of gold — and a little garment, in a small chest. But Apollo was not about to let his son die. Hermes tells how he was instructed by his brother Apollo to take the little boy to Delphi and lay him before the doors of the temple, where he was found by the Pythia, who raised him without knowledge of his ancestry. When he reached adolescence, the boy was chosen by the Delphians to be a temple servant. Since then, Hermes continues, the youth has discharged his duties happily. In Athens, meanwhile, Creusa has married Xuthus, an Achaean who once came to the rescue of the city when it was under threat of attack. So far the marriage has been without issue. In the hope of finding a remedy for their childlessness, Xuthus and Creusa have set out for Delphi to consult the oracle of Apollo.

After expounding in detail the events that have led to the action of the play, Hermes tells the audience what the course of that action will be (67–75):

> Apollo has guided destiny to this point, and has not escaped my notice, as he thinks. For he will give his own son to Xuthus when he enters this temple and will say that Xuthus is the boy's father. It is Apollo's wish that the child, coming to his mother's house, be made known to Creusa, that his affair with her remain secret, and that the child enjoy his rights. And he will lay down that he be called Ion throughout Greece, the founder of the land of Asia.

At first the action proceeds just as Apollo would have it. Xuthus receives an oracle indicating that the first person whom he encounters after leaving the temple will be his son. He encounters the youth, whom he calls Ion (cf. 661–63), and greets him enthusiastically (517ff.). At first Ion takes Xuthus for a lunatic making homoerotic advances, and he is on the point of fighting him off when Xuthus tells him about Apollo's oracle. In obedience to the word of the god, he halfheartedly embraces his new father. Up to this point Apollo's design appears to be working. Xuthus announces that he will not present Ion to his wife until they are back in Athens. She, he hopes, will agree to this remedy for their childlessness.

Euripides now effects a startling turn of events, boldly infringing one of the conventions of the Attic theater. The chorus of Athenian maidens forming Creusa's entourage does not keep secret what Xuthus has said, as the convention requires, but reports it to their mistress (760–62, 774f.). Deeply hurt by Xuthus's act of deception, Creusa follows the suggestion of her old and loyal servant, who

talks her into having Ion poisoned at the celebration that
Xuthus has organized for the son whom he feels so fortunate to have found. Fortunately, the plot miscarries. By
chance, or, as the audience may well surmise, through the
intervention of Apollo, doves sip from the poisoned wine
and die wretchedly (1122ff.). Ion enters with his retainers
to expose the author of the conspiracy. The Pythia steps
between Ion and his mother, however, and saves the day by
initiating the anagnōrismos (1320ff.). She presents to her
pupil the little chest that his mother had laid next to him
when she abandoned him. Creusa recognizes it, describes
its contents (the jewelry and the garment) to Ion, and the
son embraces his mother at last. But when his mother
tries to convince him that Apollo is his father, he is skep-
tical and sets out to consult the Delphic oracle. Suddenly
Athena appears as a dea ex machina to corroborate Creusa's
claim. Xuthus should, she says, be left in the sweet delusion that he is Ion's father (1553f.). Thus, in the end, as
Athena proclaims, Apollo has done no harm, and the
action has reached its predetermined conclusion.

The figure of Apollo, who actuates the events of the
play, has been variously interpreted. Is it Euripides' intention in *Ion* to depict a god "without character" whose conduct is reprehensible, or one whose intervention brings
about a happy conclusion?

As Hermes says in the prologue, Apollo has looked after
Ion from the beginning. He cannot be accused of neglect-
ing his child, a charge which Amphitryon, for example,
flings at Zeus in *Heracles* (339ff.). Apollo's plan would
have gone smoothly had mortals not interfered, triggering
a chain of events that the god had not foreseen. Thus,
there is a bitter truth behind the happy ending: by their
actions mortals upset the plans of the gods, and even bring
those plans to the verge of failure. The gods, on the other
hand, are not in a position to understand mortals, whose
various emotions lead to incalculable behavior; consequently, divine planning and human action seem to be all

but governed by chance, *tychē* (cf. 1512f.). In *Ion* catastrophe is averted: Ion is not killed by his mother, nor does he take revenge on her for trying to kill him. And yet there is no escaping the fact of the distance between gods and mortals.

Like *Ion, Helen* makes an altogether serious statement. As in *Heracles* and, to some extent, *Hippolytus*, a dark truth lies behind the cheerful play of appearance and reality, behind the confusion caused by the phantom and the real Helen. Two individuals, Helen and Menelaus, meet with disaster as a result of a quarrel among the gods. The human actions that are the consequence of this divine conflict turn on an illusion.

The picture of the gods drawn by Euripides, especially in *Ion*, is therefore too complex to be regarded simply as either "critical" or "pious." Those in the audience whose view of the gods was more traditional and whose religious feeling more naive would have seen their belief affirmed in the happy ending and by Athena's explanation. Those, on the other hand, who were more enlightened would have smiled in amusement at the ironic touches of the play. The appearance of Athena, goddess of the city, in the exodos and the review of Athens' earliest history would have appealed to the civic pride of every Athenian.

The importance of *Ion* in the development of European drama and, in particular, of comedy was largely due to the motifs that make up its plot: the exposed child who, in ignorance of his ancestry, lives independently under circumstances inappropriate to his birthright; the first false recognition (by Xuthus), which sets in motion an intrigue (on the part of Creusa) that functions as a counterplot (since Creusa feels that she has been deceived by her husband); the wily servant who offers his services as an accomplice in the conspiracy; the chance rescue of the victim; the rescued victim's attempt at vengeance and the avoidance of a second catastrophe through the true recognition (of mother and son) on the basis of signs; and, finally, the deceived spouse who has understood nothing of all these complications. These plot elements were fundamental to Middle and New Comedy (the fourth-century comic poet Eubulus also wrote an *Ion*) as well as of later comedy, via Plautus and Terence, and have continued to be comic mainstays up to the present day.

Drama and Mystery: *Bacchae*

Bacchae, together with *Iphigeneia at Aulis* (see p. 108) and *Alcmaeon at Corinth*, was produced after Euripides' death by a son or nephew and earned the poet posthumously one of his few victories in the tragic competition. It is one of his darkest plays and has given rise to divergent interpretations. Titles such as Norwood's *The Riddle of the Bacchae* (London, 1908) or the closing words of Karl Reinhardt's *Die Sinneskrise bei Euripides* ("To this day scholars are trying to figure out what it means"; see p. 141) illustrate the difficulties that this tragedy has posed for critics. By the beginning of the twentieth century, two opposing interpretive approaches had crystallized: some interpreted *Bacchae* as the poet's deathbed recantation, as evidence of his return to the traditional view of the gods after years of skepticism and criticism, while others saw in the play his last vitriolic indictment of the old religion, of irrational, orgiastic cults, and of the excesses of this kind of worship. All these scholars sought to discover the final "message," the legacy of Euripides. To this end, they read *Bacchae* as a tract or pamphlet rather than as a fifth-century tragedy. These anachronistic views have now been laid to rest, thanks especially to the commentary of E. R. Dodds (see p. 134). If such false notions persist, it is because critics have failed to heed the fundamental axiom governing the interpretation of a dramatic text: the statements in the play must be understood as utterances of the dramatis personae reacting to events and not as expressions of the poet's own opinion.

In making the province of the god Dionysus the central

theme of his last work, Euripides, at the end of classical Attic tragedy, harks back to the origins of the genre: the wheel has come full circle.

Several structural and formal features give *Bacchae* its retrospective orientation, its archaic quality. The chorus, which is made up of female devotees of the god, and the songs it sings are fully integrated into the dramatic action; the actor's aria, typical of Euripides' late work, is absent; the language is archaic, interspersed with Aeschylean and liturgical elements; and the so-called *antilabē* (the division of a line between two speakers) is studiously avoided (except in lines 189 and 966–70). By way of contrast to these archaic effects of language and structure, the iambic trimeter (the meter of dialogue) in *Bacchae* exhibits the increased frequency of resolution typical of Euripides' late work (43.6 percent). Consequently the "modern" rhythm of the performance is at odds with its archaic subject and creates a tension that helps to define the content of the play.

Bacchae opens with a soliloquy (the prologue of the play, 1–63). Dionysus explains that he has assumed mortal form and intends to punish those who oppose the introduction of his religion into his native city of Thebes. The sisters of his mother, Semele, are defiant, however. They allege that Dionysus was not sired by Zeus, but that Semele, on the advice of Cadmus, said that Zeus was the father to avoid the disgrace of an illegitimate child. To give proof of his divine power, Dionysus has driven the women of Thebes into a frenzy, making them leave their houses for the mountains, and in like fashion will make his power known to Pentheus, who now rules the land in Cadmus's stead, should he choose further to resist the new god.

In the scene following the entrance song of the chorus (170ff.) we see two opposing reactions to the incursion of the new divinity. First (170–209), two frail old men—the blind seer Teiresias and the erstwhile king of Thebes, Cadmus—dressed in fawnskins and equipped with thyrsus wands and ivy garlands, set out for the mountains to dance in honor of the god. Their Dionysiac costume and desire to dance are almost grotesquely incongruous with their frailness. Yet beneath the grotesquerie lies a deeper meaning: the god's power seizes even the old, the blind, and the frail.

On their way the two old men are stopped by Pentheus. The characterization of the Theban ruler is crucial to the interpretation of *Bacchae*. Is he a champion of enlightenment against an irrational and orgiastic eastern cult, which the citizens of his land are joining in droves, or simply the type of person who flouts divine power? This question is easily settled. From the beginning Pentheus's behavior is that of a typical tyrant (recalling that of Creon in *Antigone*, for example); as the exemplar of the tragic tyrant, he would have been beyond the pale of the audience's sympathy. He speaks sharply to the two old men, even threatens to have Teiresias's seat of prophecy overthrown; he regards the new cult with intransigence and prejudice; he listens neither to the arguments of Teiresias, who seeks to bring home to him the meaning of the new cult by explaining the myth of Dionysus allegorically (266ff.), nor to Cadmus, who pleads with his grandson to recognize the god, if only because it is politically judicious for the ruling family to do so (330ff.). In Pentheus's eyes, the activities of the women revelers are merely a pretext for immoderate drinking and debauchery (215ff.)

The rest of the play is taken up with Dionysus's revelation of himself as a god to Pentheus. A stranger, whom the audience knows to be Dionysus, is seized by Pentheus's henchmen and dragged before the ruler (434ff.). Pentheus's interrogation of the divine stranger shows how deepseated are his prejudices against the new cult (451ff.). At the same time the god's evasive, ambiguous answers arouse the king's curiosity (475), and his final words before he is taken away at Pentheus's behest portend the imminent catastrophe (515–18): "I am ready to go. For I am not to suffer what is not to be. Be sure, however, that Dionysus, who you say does not exist, will pursue you and make you atone for these acts of insolence. For though it is I whom you wrong, it is he whom you put in chains." Dionysus's captivity is of short duration. The earth quakes, and there is thunder and lightning. He emerges from the stables in which he was imprisoned and describes to the chorus of women revelers how the god (even for the women of the chorus he is mortal) has confounded Pentheus with hallucinations and phantoms and, to punish him for his hubris, has caused his palace to collapse into rubble (604ff.).

When Pentheus and the stranger meet again, their exchange is interrupted by a shepherd who gives an account of the activities of the women in the mountains. Despite the stranger's warning, Pentheus issues a call to arms: Thebes is to march out against the women revelers. But then Dionysus piques the king's curiosity, promising to let him observe the women secretly, on the condition that he follows him dressed like a reveler himself (810ff.). Pentheus succumbs to the temptation. The donning of the Dionysiac garb symbolizes the god's penetration into his mind.

The horrifying details of Pentheus's errand in the mountains are disclosed one by one in the final scene (1025ff.). First a servant describes how the revelers ferreted out Pentheus, and how Agave, his mother, thinking that she was hunting a lion, tore his body apart (1043ff.). In the second part of the exodos (1165ff.) Agave enters in a frenzy, holding up her son's head, which she supposes to be a hunting trophy. Just as Heracles, after the murder of his wife and children, is gradually led to see the horrible truth by his father, Amphitryon, so Cadmus leads Agave, as she awakens slowly from her delusion, to apprehend her gruesome deed (1216ff.). At this moment of extreme human suffering Dionysus appears, no longer as a mortal, but as a deus ex machina. He emphasizes that Pentheus has been punished for showing him contempt in his native city. But

whereas a deus ex machina usually, at least on a super-
ficial level, tidies up human affairs to the satisfaction of
all, Dionysus leaves the mortal characters of this play in
despair. For they cannot comprehend the workings of the
god (1348, 1381–87).

In *Bacchae*, as in *Hippolytus*, Euripides ultimately
enlists the audience's sympathy on the side of the victim.
For most of the play Pentheus represents, even more than
Hippolytus, a disagreeable, obstinate aristocrat who cannot garner any sympathy from the democratic audience.
Yet, in the end, in view of the gruesome punishment that
the god has dealt, the audience responds sympathetically
to the suffering mortal. Cadmus clearly expresses this
conflicting attitude (1341ff.). While allowing that Pentheus deserved to be punished for his impiety, the old man
accuses the god of exacting too harsh a retribution. "It
does not beseem gods," he says, "to become like mortals in
their anger" (1348). The god, however, refuses to consider
whether his revenge was justified or in due measure.
When mortals do wrong, they inevitably incur divine
punishment. In *Bacchae*, however, no one is able to see
that which, in Aeschylus, allows suffering mortals to comprehend the rational order of the gods: grace (*charis*), an
important element of Aeschylean theodicy.

If we consider only the ending of *Bacchae*, we might con-
clude that the play's theology, its expression of the distance between god and mortal, is comparable to that of
Hippolytus, Heracles, or *Orestes.* But to do so would be to
lose sight of the basic tension of the play. Dionysus
describes himself as the son of Zeus. His authority and
function are those of a god who, to mortals, can be either
extremely friendly or extremely frightening. This bipolarity of benevolence and cruelty, of joy and suffering of mortals, was originally an essential feature of his cult. For
Euripides' contemporaries, the festivals of Dionysus were
"opportunities for the mind to recover from the trials of
daily life," to quote Thucydides (2.38). The god of these fes-

tivals was benevolent and cheerful. The festivals were regimented by the polis so as to suppress the wild, primitive elements of the cult—the rending of live animals (*sparagmos*) and the eating of raw flesh (*ōmophagia*), ecstatic activities in which the revelers engaged as they roamed the mountains (*oreibasia*).

Euripides, inspired, perhaps, by his experiences in Macedonia or even by the orgiastic cults that became prevalent during the Peloponnesian War, offers in his last work an interpretation of the Dionysian in its bipolar manifestation, its overpowering beauty and attractiveness on the one hand and its inhuman cruelty on the other. It is that bipolarity of which the chorus sings in the prologue (135–69):

> He is pleasing in the mountains whenever he falls to the ground from the fleet revels, wearing the sacred dress of a fawnskin, hunting the blood of a slain goat, the joy of eating raw flesh, and hastening to the mountains of Phrygia, of Lydia: Bromius, leader of the revel, euoe! The ground flows with milk, flows with wine, flows with the nectar of honeybees. The Bacchic reveler, holding up the blazing flame of the pine torch, makes it trail from his fennel stalk like the smoke of Syrian frankincense as he runs and dances, rousing the stragglers and urging them on with his cries, tossing his delicate curls into the air. Amidst the Bacchic shouts he roars these words: "Go revelers, go revelers, pride of Tmolus that flows with gold, sing of Dionysus to the beat of the loudly sounding kettledrums, joyfully exalting the lord of joy in your Phrygian crying and screaming, whenever the melodious, sacred lotus flute sounds its sacred strains, joining you as you roam to the mountain, to the mountain!" Happily, then, the reveler gambols, guiding a swiftfooted limb, like a foal beside its dam at pasture.

APPENDIX

GENEALOGICAL TREES

The descendants of Atreus (Aeschylus's *Oresteia*; Sophocles' *Electra*; Euripides' *Electra, Orestes, Iphigeneia among the Taurians, Iphigeneia at Aulis, Helen*)

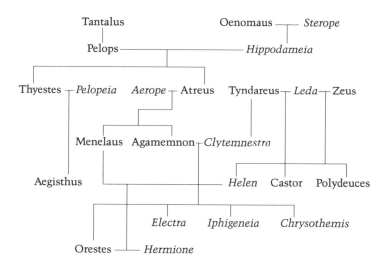

The Labdacids (Aeschylus's *Seven against Thebes*; Sophocles' *Antigone, Oedipus the King, Oedipus at Colonus*; Euripides' *Phoenician Women*)

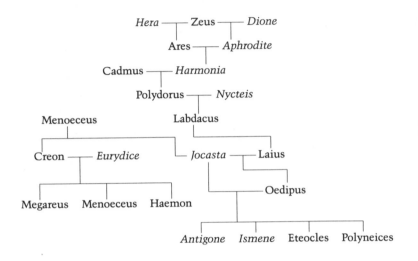

Heracles (Sophocles' *Trachinian Women*; Euripides' *Children of Heracles, Heracles*)

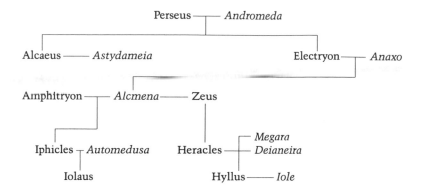

The Aeacids (Sophocles' *Ajax, Philoctetes*; Euripides' *Andromache*)

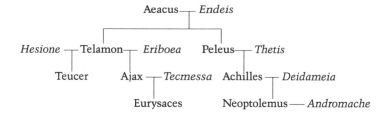

The Trojan dynasty (Aeschylus's *Agamemnon;* Euripides' *Andromache, Trojan Women, Hecuba*)

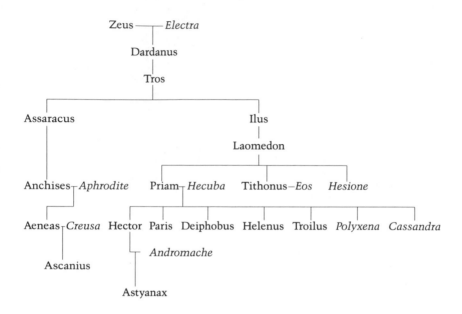

SUGGESTIONS

FOR FURTHER READING

I. Editions

Aeschyli tragoediae cum incerti poetae Prometheo, ed. M. L. West (Stuttgart, 1989).
Aeschyli septem quae supersunt tragoediae, ed. D. L. Page (Oxford, 1972).
Sophoclis fabulae, eds. H. Lloyd-Jones and N. G. Wilson (Oxford, 1990).
Sophoclis tragoediae, ed. R. D. Dawe, 2nd ed., 2 vols. (Leipzig, 1984–85).
Euripidis fabulae, 3 vols. (Oxford): vol 1, ed. J. Diggle (1984); vol. 2, ed. J. Diggle (1982); vol. 3, ed. G. Murray, 2nd ed. (1913).

A complete edition of Euripides' plays is being issued in separate volumes by the Bibliotheca Teubneriana (15 vols. to date). The fragments of Greek tragedy are available in the 5 vol. *Tragicorum Graecorum fragmenta* (Göttingen): vol. 1: *Didascaliae tragicae, catalogi tragicorum et tragoediarum, testimonia et fragmenta tragicorum minorum,* ed. B. Snell and R. Kannicht, 2nd ed. (1986); vol. 2: *Fragmenta adespota,* ed. B. Snell and R. Kannicht, 2nd ed. (1986); vol. 3: *Aeschylus,* ed. St. Radt (1985); vol. 4: *Sophocles,* ed. St. Radt (1977); vol. 5: *Euripides,* ed. R. Kannicht (forthcoming).

134

II. Commentaries (A Selection)

A. AESCHYLUS

Agamemnon: Denniston, J. D., and D. L. Page (Oxford, 1957); Fraenkel, E., 3 vols. (Oxford, 1950).
Choephori: Garvie, A. F. (Oxford, 1986).
Eumenides: Sommerstein, A. H. (Cambridge, 1989); Podlecki, A. J. (Warminster, 1989).
Persians: Broadhead, H. D. (Cambridge, 1960).
Prometheus Bound: Griffith, M. (Cambridge, 1983).
Seven against Thebes: Hutchinson, G. O. (Oxford, 1985).
Suppliants: Johansen, H. F., and E. W. Whittle (Copenhagen, 1980).

B. SOPHOCLES

Commentaries on the whole corpus: Jebb, R. (Cambridge, 1883–96); Schneidewin, F. W., and A. Nauck, ed. E. Bruhn and L. Radermacher (Leipzig, 1909–14); Kamerbeek, J. C. (Leiden, 1953–84).
Ajax: Stanford, W. B. (London, 1963).
Antigone: Müller, G. (Heidelberg, 1967).
Electra: Kells, J. H. (Cambridge, 1973).
Oedipus the King: Dawe, R. D. (Cambridge, 1982).
Philoctetes: Webster, T. B. L. (Cambridge, 1970).
Trachinian Women: Easterling, P. E. (Cambridge, 1982).

C. EURIPIDES

Alcestis: Dale, A. M. (Oxford, 1954).
Andromache: Stevens, P. T. (Oxford, 1971).
Bacchae: Dodds, E. R., 2nd ed. (Oxford, 1960).
Children of Heracles: Garzya, A. (Milan, 1958).
Cyclops: Seaford, R. (Oxford, 1984); Ussher, R. G. (Rome, 1978).
Electra: Cropp, M. J. (Warminster, 1988); Denniston, J. D. (Oxford, 1939).
Hecuba: Tierney, M. (Bristol, 1979).
Helen: Dale, A. M. (Oxford, 1967); Kannicht, R., 2 vols. (Heidelberg, 1969).

Heracles: Bond, G. W. (Oxford, 1981); Wilamowitz-Moellendorff, U. von, 2nd ed. (Berlin, 1895; repr. Darmstadt, 1959).
Hippolytus: Barrett, W. S. (Oxford, 1964).
Ion: Owen, A. S. (Oxford, 1939); Wilamowitz-Moellendorff, U. von (Berlin, 1926).
Iphigeneia at Aulis: Cesareo, G. A. (Milan, 1962).
Iphigeneia among the Taurians: Platnauer, M. (Oxford, 1938).
Medea: Page, D. L. (Oxford, 1938).
Orestes: West, M. L. (Warminster, 1987); Willink, C. W. (Oxford, 1986); Diehl, W. (Berlin, 1965).
Phoenician Women: Craik, E. (Warminster, 1988); Powell, J. U. (London, 1911; repr. New York, 1979).
Suppliant Women: Collard, C., 2 vols. (Groningen, 1975).
Trojan Women: Barlow, S. A. (Warminster, 1986); Lee, K. H. (London, 1976).

III. General

For the serious study of Greek tragedy A. Lesky, *Die tragische Dichtung der Hellenen,* 3rd ed. (Göttingen, 1972; trans. M. Dillon as *Greek Tragic Poetry* [New Haven, 1983]), is fundamental. After discussing problems of origin and pre-Aeschylean tragedy, Lesky treats all the extant plays, offering first a "descriptive analysis" of each play, in which he expounds its "plot lines, structure, and tensions" (7), and then examining its special problems. Since Lesky provides a bibliography that includes most of what has been written on tragedy before ca. 1970, the reader is referred both to his list of general works (11–16) and to the lists of special works given at the beginning of his treatment of the individual plays.

G. A. Seeck has written a concise history of the genre, in which he treats special topics such as the chorus, the idea of the tragic, and tragic theology: E. Vogt, ed., *Neues Handbuch der Literaturwissenschaft,* vol. 2, *Griechische Literatur* (Wiesbaden, 1981) 143–86. Seeck gives a more detailed account of Greek tragedy in *Das griechische Drama,* ed. G. A. Seeck (Darmstadt, 1979) 155–203. This book should be consulted by all serious students of Greek drama. It includes discussions of Aeschylus by H. Görgemanns (13–50), Sophocles by H. Diller (51–104), Euripides by K. Matthiessen (105–54), and satyr drama by B. Seidensticker

(204–57). The contributors provide succinct paraphrastic inter-pretations and focus on questions not only of form but of drama-tic technique and characterization as well.

The most recent general account of Greek tragedy is in P. E. Easterling and Bernard Knox, eds., *The Cambridge History of Classical Literature*, vol. 1, *Greek Literature* (Cambridge, 1985) 258–354, which features a full bibliography (758ff.).

Scholarly research on Greek tragedy is surveyed on a contin-ual basis in the *Anzeiger für die Altertumswissenschaft* (by H. Funke, carrying on the work of H. Strohm) and in *Lustrum* (on the fragments of Euripides, by H. J. Mette).

The current state of scholarly research is represented in a num-ber of critical anthologies.

P. Burian, ed., *Directions in Euripidean Criticism* (Durham, N.C., 1985).

H. Diller, ed., *Sophokles*, Wege der Forschung (Darmstadt, 1967).

Euripide, Entretiens sur l'antiquité classique 6 (Geneva, 1960).

Sophocle, Entretiens sur l'antiquité classique 29 (Geneva, 1983).

H. Hommel, ed., *Aischylos*, Wege der Forschung, 2 vols. (Darm-stadt, 1974).

M. H. McCall, ed., *Aeschylus: A Collection of Critical Essays* (Englewood Cliffs, N.J., 1972).

E. R. Schwinge, ed., *Euripides*, Wege der Forschung (Darmstadt, 1968).

E. Segal, ed., *Greek Tragedy: Modern Essays in Criticism* (New York, 1983), also published as *Oxford Readings in Greek Tragedy* (Oxford, 1983).

T. Woodard, ed., *Sophocles: A Collection of Critical Essays* (Englewood Cliffs, N.J., 1966).

IV. Individual Problems

A. TEXTUAL TRANSMISSION

Erbse, H., "Überlieferungsgeschichte der griechischen klassi-schen und hellenistischen Literatur," in *Die Textüberlie-ferung der antiken Literatur und der Bibel* (Munich, 1975) 207–284.

Page, D. L., *Actors' Interpolations in Greek Tragedy* (Oxford,

1934). On the corruption of the original texts through interpolations by ancient actors, and the challenge that such
interpolations pose for the modern editor.
Pfeiffer, R., *History of Classical Scholarship from the Beginnings to the End of the Hellenistic Age*, 2nd ed. (Oxford,
1968). On Hellenistic philology.

B. ORIGINS

Burkert, W., "Greek Tragedy and Sacrificial Ritual," *Greek,
Roman and Byzantine Studies* 7 (1966) 87–121. On the pre-
historic origins of tragedy.
Graf, F., *Griechische Mythologie* (Munich and Zurich, 1985) 138–
67. On the ritual and literary origins.
Winnington-Ingram, R. P., "The Origins of Tragedy," in *The Cambridge History of Classical Literature*, vol. 1, *Greek Literature*, ed. P. E. Easterling and B. M. W. Knox (Cambridge,
1985) 258–63 (with a bibliography on p. 759).

C. CONDITIONS OF PERFORMANCE AND
INSTITUTIONAL CONTEXT

Blume, H. D., *Einführung in das antike Theaterwesen* (Darmstadt, 1978).
Newiger, H.-J. "Drama und Theater," in *Das griechische Drama*,
ed. G. A. Seeck (Darmstadt, 1979) 434–503 (with a full bibliography).
Pickard-Cambridge, A., *The Dramatic Festivals of Athens*,
2nd ed. rev. J. Gould and D. M. Lewis (Oxford, 1968).
Simon, E., *Das antike Theater* (Heidelberg, 1972), trans. C. E.
Vafopoulou-Richardson as *The Ancient Theatre* (London,
1982).

The implications of the institutional context for the interpretation of Greek tragedy are discussed by W. Rösler, *Polis und
Tragödie* (Constance, 1980), who takes *Antigone* as a case in
point. On politics and Aeschylean tragedy see A. J. Podlecki, *The
Political Background of Aeschylean Tragedy* (Ann Arbor, 1966),
and C. W. Macleod, "Politics in the *Oresteia*," *Journal of Hel-
lenic Studies* 102 (1982) 122–44.

138

D. THEATER AND THEATER MACHINES

Blume, H. D.; Newiger, H.-J.; Simon E. (see Sec. IV.C above).
Hammond, N. G. L. "The Conditions of Dramatic Productions
to the Death of Aeschylus," *Greek, Roman and Byzantine
Studies* 13 (1972) 387–450.
Pickard-Cambridge, A., *The Theatre of Dionysus at Athens* (Oxford, 1946).
Pöhlmann, E., "Die Proedrie des Dionysostheaters im 5. Jahrhun-
dert und das Bühnenspiel der Klassik," *Museum Helveticum* 38 (1981) 129–46.

E. STAGECRAFT

Newiger, H.-J. (see Sec. IV.C); Hammond, N. G. L. (see Sec. IV.D).
Arnott, P. D., *Greek Scenic Conventions in the Fifth Century
B.C.* (Oxford, 1962).
Gould, J., "Tragedy in Performance," in *The Cambridge History
of Classical Literature,* vol. 1, *Greek Literature,* ed. P. E. Eas-
terling and B. M. W. Knox (Cambridge, 1985) 263–80 (with
bibliography on pp. 759–761).
Hourmouziades, N. C., *Production and Imagination in Euripi-
des* (Athens, 1965).
Melchinger, S., *Das Theater der Tragödie: Aischylos, Sopho-
cles, Euripides auf der Bühne ihrer Zeit* (Munich, 1974).
Newiger, H.-J., "Die Orestie und das Theater," *Dioniso* 48 (1977)
319–40.
Reinhardt, K., *Aischylos als Regisseur und Theologe* (Bern, 1949).
Seale, D., *Vision and Stagecraft in Sophocles* (London and Can-
berra, 1982).
Taplin, O., *The Stagecraft of Aeschylus: The Dramatic Uses of
Exits and Entrances in Greek Tragedy* (Oxford, 1977).

F. DATING

Burkert, W., "Ein Datum für Euripides' Elektra: Dionysia 420 v.
Chr.," *Museum Helveticum* 47 (1990) 65–69.
Cropp, M., and G. Fick, *Resolutions and Chronology in Euripi-
des: The Fragmentary Tragedies,* Bulletin of the Institute of
Classical Studies, suppl. 43 (London, 1985).

139

FURTHER READING

Lloyd-Jones, H., "Problems of Early Greek Tragedy," *Cuadernos de la Fundación Pastor* 13 (1966) 11–33.
Newiger, H.-J., "Elektra in Aristophanes' Wolken," *Hermes* 89 (1961) 422–430. On the revivals of Aeschylus's plays in the 420s and on the priority of the *Electra* of Euripides to that of Sophocles.
Newiger, H.-J., "Datierungsfragen der griechischen Tragödie," *Göttingische Gelehrte Anzeigen* 219 (1967) 175–94.
Müller, C. W., *Zur Datierung des sophokleischen Ödipus*, Abhandlungen der Akademie der Wissenschaften in Mainz, Geistes- und sozialwissenschaftliche Klasse 5 (1984). Müller develops a new heuristic principle for dating the plays, namely, the "assumption, based on probability and general experience, that there was an interval of two to three years between entries in the tragic competition."
Webster, T. B. L., *The Tragedies of Euripides* (London, 1967).
Webster, T. B. L., *An Introduction to Sophocles*, 2nd ed. (London, 1969).

G. STRUCTURAL ANALYSIS

Until recently, analysts of the structure of Greek tragedy have followed the traditional schematization set forth by Aristotle in his *Poetics* (1452b 14–27), according to which a tragic poem is divisible into discrete 'parts' (*merē*) — namely, prologue, episode, exodos, and choral songs (parodos and stasimon). See W. Jens, ed., *Die Bauformen der griechischen Tragödie* (Munich, 1971), in which this kind of formal analysis is still employed. Recently, a number of attempts (listed below) have been made to reorient the structural analysis of tragedy. In these studies the traditional technique, which seeks to establish a formal structure, is discarded in favor of one that recognizes a comprehensive plot structure (*systasis pragmatōn*):

Taplin, O. (see Sec. IV.E, above).
Erbse, H., *Studien zum Prolog der euripideischen Tragödie* (Berlin and New York, 1984).
Ludwig, W., *Sapheneia: Ein Beitrag zur Formkunst im Spätwerk des Euripides*, diss. (Tübingen, 1954).
Matthiessen, K., Elektra, Taurische Iphigenie und Helena: Unter-

140

suchungen zur *Chronologie und zur dramatischen Form
im Spätwerk des Euripides* (Göttingen, 1964).
Nestle, W., *Die Struktur des Eingangs in der attischen Tragödie*
(Stuttgart, 1930; repr. Hildesheim, 1967).
Seeck, G. A., *Dramatische Strukturen der griechischen Tragö-
die: Untersuchungen zu Aischylos* (Munich, 1984).

H. COMIC ELEMENTS

One topic that has received only marginal treatment in the
scholarly literature is that of the comic in Greek tragedy—that
is, comic elements and characters such as the nurse in
Aeschylus's *Choephori,* the guard in Sophocles' *Antigone,* or the
Phrygian slave in Euripides' *Orestes.* For a succinct discussion
see B. Seidensticker, *Palintonos Harmonia: Studien zu komischen Elementen in der griechischen Tragödie* (Göttingen, 1982),
and B. M. W. Knox, "Euripidean Comedy," in *Word and Action*
(Baltimore, 1979) 250–74. Aristophanic parody exploits the
comic potential of many scenes, and especially choral passages
in Euripides: see P. Rau, *Paratragodia: Untersuchungen zu einer
komischen Form des Aristophanes* (Munich, 1967).

I. THE TRAGIC HERO AND TRAGIC THEOLOGY

The modern conception of the tragic hero has been heavily
influenced by the definition given by Aristotle in chapter 13 of
his *Poetics,* according to which the hero, in order to arouse pity
and fear, must fall from a state of happiness to one of unhappiness, not because of a moral flaw, but because of a great error
(*hamartia*). Yet this definition holds true only for a limited number of plays, particularly *Oedipus the King,* which was, according to Aristotle, the ideal tragedy. See W. Söffing, *Deskriptive
und normative Bestimmungen in der Poetik des Aristoteles*
(Amsterdam, 1981) 217–25, and H. Flashar, "Die Poetik des Aristoteles und die griechische Tragödie," *Poetica* 16 (1984) 1–23. In
many plays (Aeschylus; Sophocles' *Ajax;* Euripides' *Hippolytus*)
the hero is punished for a specific crime. See H.-J. Newiger,
"Colpa e responsabilità nella tragedia greca," *Belfagor* 41 (1986)
485–99, and A. Schmitt, "Zur Charakterdarstellung des Hippolytus im Hippolytos von Euripides," *Würzburger Jahrbücher für
die Altertumswissenschaft* n. F. 3 (1977) 17–42.

141

The various ways in which the audience may see itself reflected in the tragic hero are discussed by B. Effe, "Held und Literatur: Der Funktionswandel des Herakles-Mythos in der griechischen Literatur," *Poetica* 12 (1980) 145–66, who takes the figure of Heracles in *Trachinian Women* and *Heracles* as a case in point.

Most synoptic works on Sophocles focus on the extraordinary character of the Sophoclean protagonist:

Diller, H. "Über das Selbstbewußtsein der sophokleischen Figuren: Menschendarstellung und Handlungsführung bei Sophokles," in *Kleine Schriften*, ed. H.-J. Newiger and H. Seyffert (Munich, 1971) 272–303.
Knox, B. M. W., *The Heroic Temper: Studies in Sophoclean Tragedy* (Berkeley and Los Angeles, 1964).
Reinhardt, K., *Sophokles*, 4th ed. (Frankfurt, 1976; trans. H. Harvey and D. Harvey [New York, 1979]).
Steiner, G., *Antigones* (Oxford, 1984).
Winnington-Ingram, R. P., *Sophocles: An Interpretation* (Cambridge, 1980).

That Euripides' plays subvert the heroic is argued by K. Reinhardt in his pioneering essay "Die Sinneskrise bei Euripides," in *Tradition und Geist* (Göttingen, 1960) 227–56, reprinted in *Die Krise des Helden* (Munich, 1962) 19–52 and in *Euripides*, ed. E. R. Schwinge, Wege der Forschung (Darmstadt, 1968) 507–42. Reinhardt's approach has been broadened to include the political context by W. Burkert, "Die Absurdität der Gewalt und das Ende der Tragödie: Euripides' *Orestes*," *Antike und Abendland* 20 (1974) 97–110. The view that Euripides' characters are not static but shaped by the course of the dramatic action, and susceptible to change from one scene to the next (so W. Zürcher, *Die Darstellung des Menschen im Drama des Euripides* [Basel, 1947]) is disputed by A. Lesky, "Psychologie bei Euripides," in *Euripide*, Entretiens sur l'antiquité classique (Geneva, 1960) 123–68, who detects within the characters of Euripides an inner, psychological development that is merely catalyzed as external pressure.

Any discussion of the tragic hero necessarily involves the question of the theological content of the plays. In addition to the works cited above, see the following:

Reinhardt, K. (see Sec. IV.E, above).

Wilkens, K., *Die Interdependenz zwischen Tragödienstruktur und Theologie bei Aischylos* (Munich, 1974).

Winnington-Ingram, R. P., *Studies in Aeschylus* (Cambridge, 1983).

Unlike Aeschylus, who develops a theodicy in his plays, Sophocles focuses on the distance between god and mortal and the resulting conflict between divine and mortal knowledge: see H. Diller, "Göttliches und menschliches Wissen bei Sophocles," in *Kleine Schriften*, ed. H.-J. Newiger and H. Seyffert (Munich, 1971) 255–71, and "Erwartung, Enttäuschung und Erfüllung in der griechischen Tragödie," ibid. 304–34. On the ways in which the problem of human knowledge defines the tragic see P. Szondi, "Versuch über das Tragische," *Schriften* 1 (Frankfurt, 1978) 213–18 (on *Oedipus the King*).

The deus ex machina should be mentioned in this connection. There are two interpretive approaches, which differ especially in the function that they assign to this device in the late works of Euripides. Some interpret the epiphany of the god as ironic (so W. Schmidt, *Der deus ex machina bei Euripides*, diss. [Tübingen, 1963]), while others regard it as religious (so A. Spira, *Untersuchungen zum deus ex machina bei Sophokles und Euripides* [Kallmünz, 1960]).

J. THE CHORUS

It is owing to several works by G. Müller that we have come to appreciate why Aristotle (*Poetics* 1456a 25–27) praised Sophocles for integrating the chorus into the action of his plays (see p. 22): see his "Überlegungen zum Chor der Antigone," *Hermes* 89 (1961) 398–422; "Chor und Handlung bei den griechischen Tragikern," in *Sophokles*, ed. H. Diller, Wege der Forschung (Darmstadt, 1967) 212–38; and *Sophokles: Antigone* (Heidelberg, 1967). W. Rösler, "Der Chor als Mitspieler: Beobachtungen zur Antigone," *Antike und Abendland* 29 (1983) 107–24, carries Müller's argument further (with necessary modifications). The role of the chorus in Sophocles' late plays has been investigated by Th. Paulsen, *Die Rolle des Chors in den späten Sophokles-Tragödien: Untersuchungen zu Elektra, Philoktet und Oidipus auf Kolonos*

(Bari, 1989). An overview of the chorus's function in the Sophoclean corpus is offered by R. W. B. Burton, *The Chorus in Sophocles' Tragedies* (Oxford, 1980); see also C. P. Gardiner, *The Sophoclean Chorus: A Study of Character and Function* (Iowa City, 1987). J. Rode and H. Popp have produced a typology of choral songs and lyric exchanges between chorus and actors (*amoibaia*), with due regard to the function of each within its dramatic context, in W. Jens, *Bauformen* (see Sec. IV.G) 85–116 and 221–76. For the interpretation of the metrical (that is, musical) composition of lyric passages in tragedy A. M. Dale, *The Lyric Metres of Greek Drama*, 2nd ed. (Cambridge, 1968), is fundamental. Dale is not content merely to describe and analyze the lyric passages, but ventures into interpretive metrical analysis, which inquires after the meaning and sense of the metrical form. For the principles underlying this approach see R. Kannicht, rev. of D. Korzeniewski, *Griechische Metrik*, in *Gnomon* 35 (1973) 113–34.

INDEX

Aeschylus: career of, 4, 28; dating of his plays, 28, 138–39; influence of, 46; life of, 26–27; reputation of, 27–28
— topic: hero in, 67; innovations of, 12, 44; political orientation of, 52–54; promotes ideal of civic harmony, 53–54, 58; theology (theodicy) in, 23, 33, 35, 37, 38, 40, 41, 42, 44, 45, 75, 84–85, 99, 127, 141; his trilogies thematically unified, 10. See also *anagnōrisis; stagecraft
— works: *Oresteia*, 28, 33, 36, 38–52, 104, *(Agamemnon)* 18, 19, 23, 28, 38, 39–45, 46–47, 48, 52, *(Choephori)* 28, 38, 45–49, 50, 51, 78–81, *(Eumenides)* 22, 23, 24, 28, 38, 46, 49–52, 54–55, 58, 90, 91; *Persians*, 3, 6, 15, 18, 19, 23, 26, 28, 29–33, 34, 35, 37, 52–53, 55, 112; *Prometheus Bound* (not genuine), 6, 28–29; *Seven against Thebes*, 6, 19, 23, 28, 33–35, 37, 41, 65, 107–8, 116; *Suppliants*, 5, 15, 22–23, 24, 28, 36–38, 41, 47, 66, 89, 116; lost or fragmentary plays, 11, 26, 29, 33, 36, 38
Aethiopis, epic poem, 60
Agathon, tragic poet, 4–5, 24
agōn ('contest'), agonistic nature

of tragedy, 2, 9, 12, 14 (literary oneupmanship)
aition ('account of the origin of a phenomenon'), 54, 55
Alcibiades, 105–6
Alexander of Aetolia, 5
Alexandria, Alexandrian scholars, 4–5, 136
amoibaion ('antiphonal exchange' between chorus and actor), 12, 142
anagnōrisis, anagnōrismos ('recognition'), 46–47, 79, 80, 117–18, 120, 122
antilabē (division of a line between two speakers), 124
Aphrodite, 36, 37, 57, 97–99, 102
Apollo, oracles of Apollo, 11, 33, 47, 52, 71–76, 77, 80–81, 90, 91, 104, 105, 109, 110, 111, 117, 119–21
Archelaus (king of Macedon), 86
Areopagus, 27, 54
Arion of Methymna, 7–8
aristocracy, aristocratic values, 26, 58, 61, 66, 81, 82, 94, 98–99, 102, 103, 111, 127. *See also* Areopagus
Aristophanes, 86; *Acharnians*, 88; *Birds*, 117; *Frogs*, 1–2, 6, 27–28, 87, 89; *Wasps*, 3; *Women at the Thesmophoria*, 3, 4, 88, 89
Aristophanes of Byzantium, 5, 59

147

INDEX

deus ex machina ('god from the
machine'), 13, 83–84, 96–97,
105, 110, 120, 127, 142
dialect, 7
Dionysia. See festivals of Dionysus
Dionysus: 1, 2, 6, 8, 9, 10, 11, 12,
24, 57, 123–28. See also cult
of Dionysus; festivals of Dionysus
Dioscuri (Castor and Pollux), 105
diptych, 59, 60, 70
dithyramb, 3, 7–8, 9, 10, 12, 18,
19
Dodds, E. R., 123, 134
dramatic irony, 18–19, 39, 42,
90–91, 116–18, 119, 120, 125
dreams, 30, 35, 46, 79

eavesdropping scene, 46, 79
ekkyklēma ('stage trolley'), 13, 45,
100
elpis ('hope'), 76; cf. 30, 32, 33,
62, 73, 74, 79, 85, 100, 101,
102, 103, 109, 113, 114, 120
embolima ('inserts'), 25
Ephialtes, 27, 53–54
epirrhematic composition, 23
episode, 15
epitaphios ('funeral oration'), 115
Erechtheids, 119
Erinyes, 22, 38–39, 46, 49, 52, 54,
81, 117
Eubulus, comic poet, 123
Euphorion, tragic poet, 93
Euripides: career of, 87, 93; dating of his plays, 88–89, influence of, 87, 90, 124; life of,
86–87; reputation of, 87–88
—works: Alcestis, 88, 89,
90–93; Andromache, 87, 89,
116; Bacchae, 24, 88, 123–28;
Children of Heracles, 5, 89,
115–16; Cyclops, 5, 11–12, 89;
Electra, 5, 59, 79, 80, 87, 89,

103–5, 109, 138; Hecuba, 6,
89, 108, 112–14; Helen, 5, 88,
89, 117, 122; Heracles, 5, 60,
89, 99–103, 105, 116, 122, 126,
127, 140; Hippolytus, 88, 89,
97–99, 102, 103, 122, 127, 140;
Ion, 5, 14, 20, 117, 119–22;
Iphigeneia among the Taurians, 5, 89, 117–18; Iphigeneia
at Aulis, 6, 88, 106 7, 108,
122; lost or fragmentary plays,
87, 89, 90, 97, 122; Medea, 88,
89, 93–97; Orestes, 6, 59, 80,
81, 84, 88, 89, 105–7, 109–12,
117, 127, 140; Phoenician
Women, 6, 89, 105–9, 112, 117;
Rhesus (not genuine), 88; Suppliant Women, 5, 89, 115–16;
Trojan Women, 18–19, 88, 89,
112–14, 116
—topics: as experimenter
and innovator, 87–88, 91, 97,
103, 108, 116, 120; hero as
common citizen in, 101–2,
103–5; hero subverted in, 110,
141; realism in, 87–88; skepticism in, 123; style of, 87–88;
theology in, 99, 102, 117, 121–
22, 127; treatment of women
in, 89–103. See also anagnōrisis; character development;
chorus; deus ex machina; prologue; monōidia; music; palintonos harmonia; sophists;
verbal scene painting
exodos, 15

family, familial values, 65, 69, 101,
103
festivals of Dionysus: City
(Great) Dionysia, 2, 8–9, 53,
86, 115; Lenaea, 11; organiza-
tion of City Dionysia, 9–11;
Rural Dionysia, 9
foils, 63, 68, 69, 84, 96

149